QUASARS, PULSARS, AND BLACK HOLES

opens up a world <u>where</u> . . .

Mysterious sources of light at the very limits of the observable universe shine as brightly as one hundred galaxies—and yet seem to be no bigger than our own sun.

Whole galaxies composed of anti-matter may exist—galaxies whose chance collision with our Milky Way would mean total annihilation in a cataclysmic explosion.

Black holes threaten with their awesome gravity to draw in any passing object—even the universe itself!

"Exciting and coherent. . . . Some mind-boggling —and humbling—speculations."

—*Publishers Weekly*

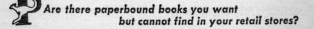

QUASARS,
PULSARS,
AND
BLACK HOLES

Frederic Golden

A KANGAROO BOOK
PUBLISHED BY POCKET BOOKS NEW YORK

QUASARS, PULSARS, AND BLACK HOLES

Scribner's edition published 1976

POCKET BOOK edition published April, 1977

This POCKET BOOK edition includes every word contained in
the original, higher-priced edition. It is printed from brand-
new plates made from completely reset, clear, easy-to-read type.
POCKET BOOK editions are published by
POCKET BOOKS,
a division of Simon & Schuster, Inc.,
A GULF+WESTERN COMPANY
630 Fifth Avenue,
New York, N.Y. 10020.
Trademarks registered in the United States
and other countries.

To
MY PARENTS

Now, my suspicion is that the universe is not only queerer than we suppose, but queerer than we *can* suppose.

J. B. S. Haldane, Possible Worlds

CONTENTS

PREFACE

As a youngster growing up in New York, I was once invited to take part in a night's stargazing sponsored by the Junior Astronomy Club which then met at the Hayden Planetarium. Under the watchful eye of a professional astronomer, we set up our small telescopes in a grassy area of Central Park known as the Sheep Meadow and pointed them at the heavens. Manhattan's dusty, light-polluted skies often cloak the brightest celestial objects. But we were lucky that night. We caught glimpses of two planets, several double stars, and even a faint galaxy.

That first youthful encounter with astronomy left an indelible mark. Though my work as a science writer requires me to delve into many different aspects of science, I still find few topics as engrossing—or as enjoyable—as astronomy. Fortunately, in the past few years, I have had every opportunity to indulge my prejudice. For hardly any other scientific area has been the setting for so many startling developments.

During this active period, I have been privileged to report many of astronomy's new discoveries, often writing about them shortly after they occurred. Yet I have found that even when the writer has the best intentions, abbreviated journalistic accounts sometimes whet the interested reader's appetite without fulfilling it. In contrast, longer and more scholarly treatments, when they eventually appear, are often no more satisfactory: they offer the nonspecialist far too much information. It was to help fill this void for the lay reader that I set out to describe, in a nontechnical way, some of astronomy's exciting breakthroughs.

Like geological strata, new scientific discoveries tend to build on the foundations of old ones. Accordingly, I have used a chronological approach. This book's early chapters are devoted to a brief review of astronomy's origins, not only to bring sweep to a majestic subject—the heavens—but to prepare the reader for more complicated concepts that follow. For instance, I have recounted the development of spectroscopy and star classification in the 19th century because the same fundamental techniques are used today to study quasars. Similarly, I have touched on such topics as the nature of the atom and fusion because they are essential to understanding how stars are formed and how they are powered.

The remainder of the book is divided into chapters that dwell on modern themes: the beginnings of radio astronomy, the pioneering work of Edwin P. Hubble, the discovery of quasars and pulsars, the first hints of the existence of black holes, and cosmological speculations about the ultimate fate of the universe. I have intentionally painted with a very broad brush; as the reader will realize, any of these subjects is so rich in material that whole books can be (and have been) written about them. Nor is this book more than an interim report on some matters. I have no doubt that in years ahead astronomers will provide totally unexpected answers to such questions as what is the real nature of quasars. Of course, some questions may never be answered—for example, will the universe's expansion ever end?

In the course of my researches on this book and my work as *Time's* science editor, I have had the pleasure of meeting or interviewing many of our most distinguished astronomers and astrophysicists, including Maarten Schmidt and Jesse L. Greenstein of the California Institute of Technology, John A. Wheeler of Princeton University, Allan R. Sandage and Halton Arp of the Hale Observatories, Carl Sagan and Thomas Gold of Cornell University, Margaret and Geoffrey Burbridge of the University of California at San Diego, Peter Strittmatter of the University of Arizona's Steward Observatory, and Riccardo Giacconi of the Harvard-Smithsonian Observatory. In spite of the demands of their busy work schedules, they all gave graciously of their time and thoughts. In addition, I am greatly indebted to Kenneth Franklin of The American Museum-Hayden Planetarium for reading the manuscript and to Graham Berry of the Caltech News Bureau for assistance in obtaining photographs and arranging visits to Palomar and Mount Wilson. I profited greatly from this help, but take sole responsibility for the pages that follow.

FREDERIC GOLDEN

INTRODUCTION

Stargazing can be the most humbling of activities. Although the earth was long considered the center of the universe, we now know that our home is only a tiny speck in space. It is one of nine major planets orbiting a star into which more than 1 million earths could fit. Our sun warms us with its life-sustaining fires, yet it too is hardly an exceptional star. Only moderate in size and already middle-aged, it is one of the 250 billion stars in a great spiral of stars called the Milky Way. Many of those stars may have planets of their own. On some of these planets conditions may have been benevolent enough for life to have evolved.

The Milky Way, for all its grandeur, is not extraordinary either. It is just one of millions upon millions of such collections of stars, or galaxies (from the Greek word for "milk"). Even the closest galaxies are very far apart; it takes light from the neighboring galaxy in Andromeda, a spiral like our own Milky Way, more than 2 million years to reach us, even though light travels at 186,000 miles per second, or some 6 trillion miles in a year. Yet Andromeda is, cosmically speaking, next door; it is a member of the same local group of galaxies as the Milky Way.

Other clusters are vastly more distant. In the great

200-inch telescope atop Palomar mountain in California, astronomers have spotted galaxies and clusters a thousand times more distant than Andromeda. Indeed, our universe is so vast, so far-flung, that its immense size is almost beyond ordinary comprehension. Even if we tried to travel only a short distance out of the solar system, the journey would take longer than the lifetime of a single astronaut or of several generations of astronauts. Our fastest existing rockets could not carry us to the nearest star beyond the sun, Proxima Centauri, which is only 4.3 light-years away, in less than many hundreds of years. If we tried to go farther—say, on an expedition across the galaxy (which is 100,000 light-years in diameter)—it would take us millions of years.

The witty British theologian and science fiction writer C. S. Lewis liked to speak of these great distances as "God's quarantine." In Lewis's view, they were intentionally designed to keep a less-than-perfect species (ourselves) from contaminating other worlds —and other beings—that may have achieved a purer state. Yet in spite of such a barrier, science has lately been able to explore the heavens in incredible detail, even without venturing far from the earth, and has revealed many of the secrets of those distant worlds.

Some of the information has been gathered by rockets and orbiting satellites; operating above the earth's thick blanket of air, these instruments can see clearer and farther than those based on the ground underneath the obscuring atmosphere. Considerable data have also been obtained by the first landings on the moon, a celestial body that has remained largely unchanged in billions of years and thus offers vital clues to the origin and history of the solar system. In contrast, on earth wind, rain, and other geological processes have largely wiped out these signs. Finally, there has been an extraordinary burst of knowledge from unmanned probes into the solar system that have explored all the plants out to Jupiter.

Meanwhile, astronomers have not been inactive on

earth. By using such products of modern electronic wizardry as computers and televisionlike image intensifier tubes, they have vastly expanded the power of traditional observational tools. The American astronomer Jesse L. Greenstein, for instance, points out that such improvements now enable the 200-inch Palomar mirror to do work that once would have required a 600-inch telescope. In addition, astronomers have opened whole new windows on the universe by looking at signals—radio waves, X rays, and, according to some scientists, even long-elusive gravitational waves—that were all but undetectable a few decades ago.

As a consequence of the introduction of these new tools and techniques, our view of the universe has been totally revolutionized. It is not only incredibly larger, but vastly different from earlier conceptions. As late as the 19th century, many astronomers thought of the universe as a serene place where the stars shone with reassuring permanence and the planets moved with clocklike regularity. Now we know otherwise. The universe is not tranquil or static, but disturbed by events of awesome violence. Stars explode with unimaginable fury and whole galaxies are ripped apart. Swirling magnetic fields many times stronger than the earth's whip particles through space at greater energies than those achieved by our most powerful particle accelerators. Yet in the midst of such chaos, there is a semblance of order. Molecules are formed, and scientists have even found hints that the first tentative biochemical steps that led to the emergence of life on earth may be taking place in the vast, hostile regions between the stars.

Our new view has also revealed great mysteries. As astronomers look far off into space, they detect baffling blurs of light and radio waves. This prodigious energy has apparently traveled over enormous distances from puzzling objects called quasars (for quasistellar), or starlike bodies, which in fact do not seem to be stars at all. On the contrary, they may well be something entirely different: the most distant—and ancient—objects in a universe that most astronomers believe was born billions of years ago in the great explosion called the Big Bang. If they are indeed so far off, perched at the very "edge" of the known universe, they would have to be shining a hundred times brighter than a galaxy of billions of stars to be seen on earth. Yet quasars do not seem to be much bigger than our solar system. What great energy source powers these distant candles?

In contrast, astronomers have partly solved the mystery of another dramatic new discovery. First thought to be the beacons of a distant civilization when they were detected in 1967, pulsars (for pulsating star) are now known to be a natural phenomenon, which astronomers initially refused to believe could exist: so-called neutron stars, the cadavers of stars even larger than the sun that have compressed themselves into a ball no more than a few miles across.

But even neutron stars are apparently not the ultimate form of stellar collapse. Many astronomers are convinced that more compact objects exist. In effect, their matter is so thoroughly squeezed that it is crushed into oblivion; hence they are called black holes, which are literally points of nothingness in space. Amazingly, even though black holes give off no light, astronomers think that they have detected the presence of at least one such object by ingenious scientific detective work.

But many questions still remain. If black holes are really remnants of matter that has completely vanished from view, where has it gone? Could it have tunneled into another part of the universe, or perhaps into a different universe? And what of our own universe? Since the 1920s, astronomers have known that it is expanding, with all its galaxies flying apart. Is it possible that sometime in the future this expansion will reverse itself and all the parts of the universe will come crashing together, perhaps also crushing itself out of existence? Incredible as they may seem, such

ideas are now being considered with utmost serious-
ness by the most thoughtful scientists.

In the eyes of many astronomers, the past few
years have been one of the most exciting interludes in
the history of their venerable science. Some of them,
like Greenstein, consider it a new golden age of
astronomy. And they point out that there has been
nothing quite like it since the Polish churchman-
astronomer Nicolaus Copernicus dethroned the earth
from its central position in the solar system more
than four centuries ago or since that starry night in
Venice half a century later when Galileo Galilei
showed the elders of the city the "seas" of the moon
and the moons of Jupiter through his new telescope.
Like those earlier periods, the new era of discovery
has opened new vistas and posed great new puzzles.

QUASARS,
PULSARS,
AND
BLACK HOLES

1

THE BEGINNINGS
OF STARGAZING

Astronomy is perhaps the oldest of sciences, older than the study of the human body or the first systematic planting and harvesting of grains. It traces back to the first time humans gazed at the heavens and wondered what secrets they held. Possibly they pondered such questions as how the universe began and what it was made of, but they also had a more down-to-earth motive for looking up into the star-filled night.

As long as 20,000 or 30,000 years ago, even before the first agricultural societies arose, Ice Age cave dwellers were using the changing face of the moon— its phases—to mark the passage of time. Such knowledge was extremely important to their survival. It enabled them to predict the seasons, and thus await the migration of the herds of animals they hunted for food. As they turned from hunting to cultivation of crops, the ability to anticipate the seasons accurately became even more valuable. If they failed to sow their seeds at the proper time of the year, the prospects for a bountiful harvest would dim considerably.

The reason that the moon, sun, and stars make such good calendars is that their motions across the sky are calculable. Even with relatively primitive devices, they can be measured and predicted. It seems difficult to believe that ancient peoples had such skills, but they have left behind considerable evidence of their astronomical capabilities. On Salisbury Plain in southern Britain stands a great circular monument known as Stonehenge. Its construction began some four thousand years ago during the Bronze Age, and its ancient builders managed to align the monument's great slabs of stone so well that their positions can still be used to foretell the day the midsummer sun will rise. The British-born astronomer Gerald Hawkins has suggested a more controversial idea: that the priests who ran this ancient observatory could even predict eclipses, which were then events of great foreboding.

Astronomical knowledge was not limited to the Old World. Certainly, the Indians of prehistoric America studied the heavens and occasionally noted what they had seen. In the jungles where the present-day borders of Brazil, Peru, and Bolivia meet, the American archaeologist George Michanowsky has recently found rock carvings that may represent the explosion of a star as many as ten thousand years ago. Farther south, along the coastal plain of Peru, long lines and great figures, some of them hundreds of feet in length, have been carved into the floor of the Nazca valley; about a thousand years old, these markings are so accurately laid out that they form pointers to certain stars. The entire valley may have been used by the Indians as an astronomical observatory. To the north, in Central America, the Mayans had not only mastered language and engineering skills comparable to the Egyptians', but also managed a good enough understanding of planetary motion to keep an accurate calendar.

Across the seas in China, astronomers had long been an important part of the life of the royal court. The emperor not only expected his court astronomers to advise him when the stars were in favorable positions, but could be unduly harsh when they neglected their duties. According to accounts of the time, the court astronomers Hi and Ho were summarily beheaded when they failed to predict an eclipse in 2159 B.C. They had apparently been too busy drinking.

The Chinese could perhaps dispute the claim, but the first true astronomers in a modern sense were the Chaldeans, an ancient people of Babylonia, who dwelled in the heart of the Fertile Crescent region in present-day Iraq. They looked to the skies not only to seek omens of the gods' favor or disfavor, but simply for the joy of learning more about them. Even so, they made no distinction between their more scientifically rigorous stargazing and their interest in astrology, which holds that our daily lives and fortunes are directly under the influence of the heavens. In this respect, the Chaldeans were no different from other ancient peoples, including the Egyptians, Persians, and Greeks. All of them were certain that the heavens were populated by powerful gods and goddesses who did much to direct the fate of the lesser beings on earth. But these gods displayed surprisingly human foibles as they fought, schemed, and wooed each other in their celestial abode. Indeed, one can easily imagine ancient storytellers sitting on a hillside on a clear, starry night, spinning out yarns about the gods before enthralled audiences. The heavens were the television of the time, an enormous source of entertainment.

In the winter skies above the Mediterranean area, the ancients identified the most conspicuous constellation of stars as Orion, the mighty hunter. In his midriff, three bright stars formed his belt; another group of stars were his sword. In his hand, Orion held a club, which he was using to ward off the charging bull Taurus, a nearby constellation. To his rear, Orion was followed by his two hunting dogs, Canis Major and Canis Minor, which were pursuing Lepus the hare, another constellation. The larger dog's eye was a particularly bright star, Sirius, otherwise known as the Dog Star. (Astronomers now know that Sirius is actually two stars: a so-called binary—or twin—star system in which the two members revolve about each other.)

Watching these celestial figures provided not only amusement but vital information. The Egyptians eagerly awaited the rising of Sirius each year just before the sun in the predawn sky. For the star's reappearance was a sign that the life-giving waters of the Nile, so essential for irrigation, were about to flood, as they had every year as far back as anyone could recall. The ancient Persians, for their part, looked upon Sirius as Tishtrya, the great rain god who vanquished Apaosha, the demon of drought. But the Greeks did not seem impressed with Sirius. With their characteristic scientific logic, they assumed that when Sirius dropped out of sight into the sun's bright glare, it was adding its rays to those of the sun. According to the Greeks, that meant a long, hot summer.

While gazing at the stars, the ancients also recognized differences between them. As the great dome of the heavens appeared to rotate, most stars seemed to remain fixed in the same spot relative to other stars in their vicinity. But some stars moved across the sky with a motion independent of it. The Greeks called these moving stars "planets," or wanderers. In all they counted seven planets—Mercury, Venus, Mars, Jupiter, and Saturn, as well as the sun and moon. Some ancient peoples thought that the stars were great lanterns suspended in the vault of the heavens, like candles in a great domed building. Others said that they were holes cut into the celestial sphere behind which great fires raged.

To account for the independent motion of the planets, Greeks devised a more elaborate conception. According to their great astronomer Ptolemy, the heavens were made up of rotating concentric crystal spheres nestled in each other like bowls. The stars were embedded in the outermost sphere, while inner spheres held the sun, moon, and other planets. It was a scheme in total harmony with the Greek idea that the circle was the most perfect of geometric forms. At the center of this universe was the earth.

Ptolemy's ideas held sway for some 1500 years, all through the Middle Ages, which shows what a remarkable theory it was. Yet, as navigators needed more accurate star positions for their long voyages, more and more errors began to crop up. The Ptolemaic system was unable to predict the movements of the planets with adequate precision. To make theory fit observations, astronomers suggested that the planets made smaller loops within the larger circles. But they created such a complex system that Ptolemy's spheres no longer seemed an adequate explanation for heavenly motions.

Reluctantly and after at least twenty years of work, Nicolaus Copernicus published a small, dryly mathematical text, *De Revolutionibus Orbium Coelestium* (On the Revolutions of the Heavenly Orbs) in 1543 when he lay on his deathbed. Copernicus's caution was understandable. In one brilliant stroke, he overturned the Ptolemaic system, which had the earth at the center of the universe, and replaced it with one in which the earth was merely part of a central sun's family of planets. Along with the earth, man was demoted, an idea that challenged prevailing theological orthodoxy.

At first, those who espoused the Copernican view did so only at considerable risk. One of Copernicus's more ardent champions was the Italian monk Giordano Bruno, who was burned at the stake for suggesting such heretical ideas as the possibility that the sun might be an ordinary star like the others in the sky. An even more effective advocate of the Copernican universe was Galileo Galilei, whose writings in support of it so infuriated the pope that the aged scientist was tried, even though he was nearly 70 years old, and placed under house arrest for the remainder of his life. Yet all the power and influence of the church authorities could not save the faltering Ptolemaic idea that the earth was the hub of the universe.

Nothing did more to bury Ptolemy's earth-centered system than the introduction of a remarkable new optical instrument. Invented by spectacle makers in Flanders in late 1608, the telescope had been quickly turned to the skies by Galileo. Although his instrument had no more magnification power than an ordinary pair of present-day binoculars, it led to a discovery that strongly supported the Copernican theory. Gazing at the giant planet Jupiter, Galileo found that it was surrounded by four moons, which orbited the planet just as the Copernican theory supposed that the planets, including the earth, orbited the sun. In short, Jupiter and its satellites comprised a miniature solar system.

The new telescope also revealed other wonders. Galileo found that the moon's surface was covered by craters and what he mistakenly thought were *maria* (or seas), which suggested at least vague similarities between earth and moon. He also discovered that the planet Venus underwent phases, like the moon; sometimes the entire disk of the planet could be seen, at others it appeared as a silvery crescent. Such observations could not readily be explained by a system in which the sun was in orbit around the earth. Finally, Galileo's telescope showed that the Milky Way consisted of many stars closely packed together. Clearly, these observations hinted at a universe far more complex and varied than that envisioned by the ancients.

Copernicus's theory itself had flaws. Like Ptolemy, he had his celestial bodies moving in circles. In fact, as was shown by Galileo's German contemporary Johannes Kepler, they move in ellipses. But in its overall view the Copernican system was not only basically correct, but—with the Keplerian corrections—profoundly revolutionary. It led directly to formulation of the theory of gravity by Britain's Sir Isaac Newton, which could tell astronomers for the first time where any body in the solar system should be at any particular time, with uncanny accuracy. The solar system was no longer a mystical entity guided by the whims and caprices of the gods.

Precisely obeying Newton's laws, the separate parts of the solar system moved like the finely machined parts of a clock. Every planet had to follow a precisely calculable path; any deviation from the system had to have a cause. Spreading its influence throughout the solar system, gravity reigned supreme in Newton's clockwork universe. When the planet Uranus was found by 18th-century astronomers to be straying from the pathway predicted by Newton's laws, they searched for whatever was pulling Uranus off course. The hunt led to the discovery of another planet, Neptune, at preciscly the point in space where Newtonian theory had said astronomers should find it.

The Copernican revolution was complete. Equipped with their new theories of the universe and a new tool to examine it, astronomers began exploring the heavens with an enthusiasm and intensity unmatched in any earlier age. Their quest soon produced unexpected results.

2

THE NATURE
OF STARLIGHT

Even after the invention of the telescope early in the 17th century, astronomers were far more concerned with the moon, planets, and the sun than with the more distant stars. The reason was not entirely indifference on their part. On the contrary, no matter how hard they looked at the stars, they were no more than pinpoints of light. In contrast, even in the first low-powered telescopes the planets appeared as disks. At times the view was so good that astronomers could recognize surface features—for instance, the great red spot of Jupiter. The upshot was that astronomers occasionally studied stars to determine their position and motion, but did not give much thought to what they were.

It was only after another experiment by Newton that astronomers could explore the nature of stars. Letting a beam of sunlight enter his darkened study at Cambridge University through a small hole in his window shutters one day in 1666, Newton aimed the rays through a prism. The light did not emerge from the triangular-shaped piece of glass as a single white beam.

Instead, it appeared on the opposite wall as a brilliant rainbow of colors. Like all rainbows, the light contained seven hues—red, orange, yellow, green, blue, indigo, and violet—each merging into the next in a definite order.

Newton called the rainbow a spectrum (after the Latin word for "ghost") and, unlike others who had tried similar experiments, he immediately recognized the significance of his little test. Even though sunlight normally appears white, it is a mix of colors. The same effect occurs when sunlight passes through droplets of water or bounces off the angled glass of a crystal chandelier. But no one understood the phenomenon until Newton provided an explanation.

From his work, he concluded that light consisted of tiny particles ("corpuscles") of different color. The particles normally traveled so fast that they appeared almost instantaneous and thus could not be distinguished from one another. But when they moved from one substance to another—say, from air to glass—their velocity was differently affected. Some slowed down more than others. To use Newton's word, each color had a different "refrangibility." Thus, as various particles passed through the glass, they were also bent at a different rate—the violet end of the spectrum bending more than the red.

Some scientists objected to Newton's explanation of light. They wondered why, if light consisted of particles, some should have different speeds from others. Moreover, they asked how could two beams, made of Newton's corpuscles, collide without canceling each other out. In fact, the evidence showed quite the contrary: two beams usually tended to enhance each other.

The 17th-century Dutch scientist Christian Huygens gave a bold answer to these paradoxical questions. He said that Newton's theory was wrong, and that light consisted of waves, like ripples in a rope. The length of each wave was measured by the distance between successive high or low points. Thus the different colors were the result not of different particles but of varying wavelengths. According to Huygens's wave theory, light's speed still changed in different substances. But the amount of bending for different colors depended on their wavelengths.

Huygens's explanation met certain objections to the Newtonian particle theory, such as the problem of the intersecting beams. But it too left key questions unanswered. It did not explain, for instance, why light waves, unlike water or sound waves, could not go around obstacles. Nor did it account for how light could travel as waves through the apparent emptiness of space from the sun or stars to the earth. The waves had to be vibrating in some medium. Later scientists tried to resolve this problem by conjuring up a substance called the ether which they said filled all of space.

For a long time, scientists were divided on the nature of light. The larger group espoused Newton's corpuscle theory, at least partly because of his great prestige. Others sided with Huygens, insisting that light had to consist of waves. As so often happens in science, there was truth on both sides. But it was not until the beginning of the 20th century that this paradoxical situation was recognized. In his special theory of relativity, the German-born physicist Albert Einstein put forth the incredible proposition that light had characteristics of both waves and particles. Contradictory and controversial as this idea seemed in 1905 when Einstein announced it, the dual nature of light is now recognized by scientists as one of the basic tenets of modern physics.

Even though Newton's corpuscle theory was only partly correct, it was sufficiently useful to solve a nagging difficulty for astronomers of his day. Up to that time, all telescopes produced rings of color around the objects under study. Newton's experiment showed why: the lenses of the telescope acted like prisms, breaking up the incoming light into the annoying rings. To eliminate them Newton designed a totally new type of telescope. It magnified the light not by an ordinary lens but by a curved mirror. Reflecting the light rather than letting it pass through the glass, the device was essentially ring-free (although some color disturbance still occurred at the eyepiece where the reflected light from the mirror came together). In this way, Newton invented the reflector telescope, which today is still the most popular type of instrument, especially when there is a need for great light gathering.

Lens makers subsequently devised a way to eliminate the rings without resorting to a mirror. By 1757 the English optician John Dolland had shown that two lenses of different kinds of glass when properly fitted together canceled out each other's spectra. His breakthrough revived interest in so-called refracting telescopes, using see-through lenses, and eventually they grew quite large in size. Today the largest telescope of this type is the 40-inch refractor of the University of Chicago's Yerkes Observatory near Williams Bay, Wisconsin. (The size of a telescope is measured by the diameter of its principal lens or mirror.) But bigger refractors become impractical for two reasons: first, lenses are more difficult to grind than mirrors because they have two surfaces; and second, large lenses absorb much of the light that passes through them. So, for the biggest telescopes, astronomers continue to favor reflectors over refractors.

Newton's prism experiment led to a second major development for astronomy. In effect he had devised the first spectroscope; this is an instrument that breaks up light into its various component colors. But before the device could be really useful to astronomers anxious to study the light from stars, it required a subtle refinement. That was achieved by the early-19th-century German optician Joseph von Fraunhofer when he repeated Newton's experiment with a slight variation. Before letting the beam of incoming light strike the prism, he passed it through a narrow slit. As a result, each spectral color was projected as a separate image of the slit. A highly skilled craftsman, Fraunhofer produced such sharp images that he could see that at certain places in the spectrum of sunlight there was little or no light. Working with methodical care, Fraunhofer eventually mapped seven hundred such dark bands in the spectrum of sunlight. These are called Fraunhofer lines in honor of their discoverer.

Scientists soon suspected the significance of the lines, but it was only after the work of two other Germans, the 19-century chemists Wilhelm Bunsen and Gustav Kirchhoff, that their suspicions were confirmed. Bunsen and Kirchhoff heated many substances to a glow and used spectroscopes to study the light they gave off. What they learned was that each substance had its characteristic spectral lines. Eventually they became so skilled at such analysis that they could identify elements simply by heating them and looking at their various colors.

Such displays are called emission spectra for the obvious reason that they are produced by the emission of light from objects heated to incandescence. Scientists also discovered another kind of spectrum. If something is placed between the glowing object and the spectroscope—say, a hot gas—some of the original source's light will be removed or absorbed. The result is one or more dark bands of the kind Fraunhofer first observed. These are known as absorption spectra since they are caused by absorption of some of the original light.

The conclusion from these experiments was quite plain: every substance produced its characteristic light. Furthermore, under the right conditions, the telltale spectra could be used like fingerprints to distinguish between substances.

The spectroscope proved invaluable for astronomers. At last they had an instrument that could give them clues to what stars are made of. All they had to do was to compare known spectral lines, determined by studies in the laboratory, with the unknown spectra of light from the stars. Indeed, once they began fitting spectroscopes to their telescopes, they found that identifying the major components of the sun and stars was almost

as easy as if they had the distant bodies in their own
backyards.

Discoveries came rapidly. As early as 1862, the
Swedish astronomer Anders Jonas Ångström (whose
name is now used as a unit to measure the wavelength
of light) found hydrogen on the sun. During an eclipse
a few years later, the French astronomer Pierre Jules
César Janssen sighted a spectral line in the light from
the sun's chromosphere (or lower atmosphere) that
was completely unfamiliar. The British astronomer Sir
Norman Lockyer promptly concluded that a new element had been discovered and named it helium after
the Greek word for the sun *(helios)*. In 1895 the
element was finally found on earth, providing a stunning triumph for the new science of spectroscopy.

Spectroscopic observations not only revealed the
composition of stars. They also enabled astronomers to
estimate for the first time their surface temperatures,
since all elements change color in a predictable way
when they are heated. Iron, for instance, initially turns
red, then orange and yellow, and finally white as its
temperature is increased in a furnace. During the heating, iron's spectrum changes so that the brightest visible color at any moment will also be its most conspicuous component. The astronomer thus can tell stellar
temperature by comparing the intensity of the various
colors in a star's spectrum.

The spectroscope also told astronomers something
about a star's movements. The principle involved in
such measurements was first explained by the 19th-
century Austrian physicist Christian Doppler, who
compared it to a familiar earthly phenomenon. When
a train approaches an observer on a station platform,
its whistle seems to rise in pitch; as the train pulls out
of the station, the pitch appears to go down. Doppler
realized that the pitch of the whistle itself had not
changed; it emits sound waves at a steady frequency
(that is, the number of waves given off by the whistle
during any period remains the same). What happens

is that when the train approaches the station platform, the whistle's sound waves crowd up so that more are hitting the observer's eardrum at any given moment. As a result for the observer, the whistle's pitch has risen, since pitch goes up with frequency. Conversely, as the train pulls away, the sound waves are stretched out. Fewer waves strike the observer's ear at any moment, and the whistle's pitch goes down. Instead of a shrieking high-pitched whine, he hears the train's whistle as a long, low wail.

The Doppler effect should also apply to light, whose waves (or particles) would also pile up or stretch out depending on the motion of the light's source. It was the French physicist Armand Fizeau who first pointed out, in 1848, how such movements could be observed in a star's spectrum. If the star is moving toward the earth, the frequency of its light will be increased, pushing the spectral lines to the blue (or higher frequency) end of the spectrum. Astronomers call the phenomenon a blue shift, and they can use it to measure the velocity of a heavenly body toward the earth. If the star is moving away from the earth, the frequency of its light will decrease and its spectral lines will be moved to the red (or lower) end of the spectrum. Hence, the star's light is said to be red-shifted, and the extent of the shift can be used to clock the star's speed away from us.

Equally important, the spectroscope was able to tell astronomers something about a star's size and distance. As noted earlier, telescopes show stars only as pinpoints of light; even the 200-inch Palomar telescope cannot resolve stars into anything more than flecks on a photographic plate—although new computer techniques may be able to give astronomers better stellar images in the future. Thus astronomers had no accurate way to estimate the diameter of stars except by their relative brightness, the assumption being that the brighter the star, the bigger it is. But such estimates can be highly misleading.

Differences in the brightness of stars may also be due

to their relative distances from earth. A star may only seem brighter than another star because it is closer rather than larger. How, then, can you determine the star's true brightness—or absolute magnitude, in the astronomer's language—apart from its distance? The spectroscope provided the answer, since the analysis of the star's spectral lines also gives a good indication of its real brightness. With that information, astronomers could go on to calculate a star's distance.

Before the introduction of the spectroscope, astronomers relied mainly on a trigonometric scheme known as parallax for distance measurements. It involves measuring the apparent shifting of a star's position as the earth moves around the sun. The technique is akin to a game sometimes played by youngsters. If they hold a pencil about a foot in front of their noses, then look at it successively with one eye and then the other, the pencil will appear to jump back and forth. If the little game is repeated with the pencil held about two feet away, it will still move back and forth, but much less. Anyone playing this game soon realizes that the pencil's movements are directly related to its distance from the observer's nose.

Astronomers can play the same game with stars. By comparing a star's position in the summer, say, when the earth is on one side of the sun, with its position in the winter, when the earth is on the other side, they can measure the star's distance with remarkable precision. The trouble is that the technique works only for relatively close stars. Beyond 100 light-years, parallax measurements become increasingly unreliable even with the most powerful telescopes.

As early as the 18th century the great German-born English astronomer William Herschel thought that he could use a star's brightness as a yardstick of distance. The underlying assumption he made was that all stars are more less equally bright, like candles of equal glow. Only their varying distances, he reasoned, made them seem brighter or dimmer. Consequently, a star that was a fourth as bright as its neighbor should be twice as distant. Herschel's reckoning is based on a well-known law of physics: the brightness of an object diminishes as the square of its distance—that is, the distance multiplied by itself. But this apparently foolproof approach did not work very well, at least not in Herschel's day. Contrary to his assumption, stars differ enormously in absolute magnitude. Some stars called supergiants, for instance, have been discovered to be a million times brighter than the sun. It was only when spectroscopy became available as a tool for estimating absolute stellar brightness that astronomers could put Herschel's yardstick to work with expectations of getting reasonably accurate results. Thus spectroscopy finally gave astronomy the means to measure the distance of faroff stars.

The spectroscope eventually revealed other mysteries about stars—whether they had magnetic fields, whether they were single or double stars, even whether they were young or old. By the end of the 19th century, in fact, the instrument had yielded so much information that the only way astronomers could cope with it was to begin classifying stars by type. As their basic guideline they used the star's surface temperature, and stars of roughly the same temperature were designated by the same letter. Astronomers used ten letters: O, B, A, F, G, K, M, R, N, S, each representing a different temperature range; O stars are the hottest, S the coolest. (For countless students of astronomy, the easiest way to learn these letters has been to memorize a famous sentence: "Oh, Be A Fine Girl, Kiss Me Right Now, Sweet!") The designers of this spectral classification scheme originally intended to make their list alphabetical—A, B, C, and so on—but soon errors were discovered. Some O stars, for example, were found to be unexpectedly hot; eventually they were placed ahead of the B class. To complicate matters, astronomers found large temperature differences in the same groups. That forced them to divide the original classifications into ten subgroups—for instances, B-0, B-1, B-2, and so forth.

In the groupings, the sun ranked somewhere in the middle; it was a star of G-2 spectral class, which indicated a star of moderate temperature, brightness, and size. Sirius, the brightest star in the night sky, has a designation befitting its great luminosity: A-0.

What made this accumulation of information even more significant was another 19th-century innovation that let astronomers study starlight long after they initially glimpsed it through the eyepieces of their telescopes. That innovation was photography. Soon after the French artist Louis Daguerre introduced his daguerreotypes in 1830, astronomers adapted the new technique. Herschel's son John was one of the first to experiment with photography. By the 1880s, the American Henry Draper had managed not only to photograph the moon and several nebulas (clouds of gases or stars) but to record on his plates the spectra of a number of individual stars.

The importance of photography to the advance of astronomy cannot be overestimated. Before its introduction, astronomers could only sketch what they saw —or thought they saw, since the eye often plays tricks on the observer—through their telescopes. The results, as might be expected, were often less than accurate. Photographic plates, by contrast, leave a virtually flawless record. Moreover, photography can be used to observe exceptionally faint objects like galaxies. As the telescope tracks such distant blurs, often for hours at a time, their light, in effect, accumulates on the film, producing an image that might not be seen by an observer looking through the eyepiece for a few moments.

All these developments occurred within a rather short span, and they caught even the most sophisticated scientists by surprise. Midway in the 19th century, the French philosopher Auguste Comte had speculated about what kinds of knowledge would never be attained by science. As an example, he chose the chemical makeup of stars. Yet only a few years later, as a result largely of the new insights derived from the combination of spectroscopy and photography, astronomers had learned the basic composition of the sun as well as that of far more distant stars.

Still, great questions remained unanswered. Despite astronomy's new tools, no one could really explain how stars burn, or how they are formed, or how long they will endure. Soon astronomers would provide answers, but in that quest they would also turn up many new mysteries about the universe.

3

THE THERMONUCLEAR FIRES

Nothing seems more permanent than the stars. If an ancient Greek stargazer could look into our nighttime sky, he would be hard put to notice many differences in the configuration of the heavens from his day. The few that he might spot would be rather minor, resulting from the earth's wobble on its axis. Indeed, his observations might confirm his conviction that the celestial "spheres" were perfect and, in the main, unchanging. Whatever changes did occur were assigned, in any event, to the lowest sphere, which held the moon and was the least important.

Even when the evidence was against them, the Greek philosophers were inflexible. Aristotle, so perceptive in other areas, firmly insisted that comets were fiery "exhalations" in the atmosphere—although their slow movement, as opposed to that of streaking meteors, indicated that comets were far more distant objects. Some Greeks, of course, had distinctly modern ideas. Two millennia before Copernicus, Aristarchus of Samos was arguing that the earth and other planets traveled around the sun. But he was a distinctly minority voice; for all their stargazing skill, the Greeks remained blind to the obvious. Nothing in their surviving records, for example, hints of the existence of variable stars, some of which, like Algol in the constellation Perseus, the Prince (after the son of the god Zeus), display changes in luminosity that are apparent without telescopes. (Now we know that Algol has a smaller companion that passes in front of it every sixty-nine hours, partly eclipsing its light.)

There was one heavenly event that the Greeks could not ignore. It was the sudden appearance of a "new" star. Spotting such a bright newcomer in the constellation Scorpius (the scorpion), in 134 B.C., the philosopher Hipparchus was so awed that he noted the star's position on a chart. His map is thought to be the first sky chart of its kind, and was specifically drawn by him so that other new stars could be more readily identified when they appeared in the future.

Now we know that such new stars, or novas—as they were called by the Danish astronomer Tycho Brahe in the 16th century—are not new at all. They are really very ancient stars that momentarily flare up in their death throes. But such insights into stellar behavior are quite modern. It is only in the past few decades that astronomers have begun to understand how stars evolve, continue burning for millions—even billions—of years, and then die.

The most obvious place to look for answers to questions about such stellar enigmas is the nearest star. As early as 1848 a young German physician named Julius Mayer wondered what powered the sun. Others had already suggested that it was a huge lump of burning coal. But Mayer's calculations showed that even a lump of coal as large as the sun would be nothing but ashes in less than five thousand years. By Mayer's day, geological evidence had already suggested that the earth—and thus the entire solar system—was much older. So Mayer looked for another solar energy source. He contrived an ingenious theory; he suggested that the sun was under continual bombardment by meteoroids. As these small chunks of interplanetary debris fell into the sun, they provided a continual supply of fuel for the sun's fires. But other scientists quickly saw the flaw in Mayer's thesis. To stoke the sun's great fires to the required temperatures would have needed far more meteoroids than are known to exist in the sun's vicinity or anywhere else in the solar system.

In 1854 the German physicist Hermann Ludwig Ferdinand von Helmholtz proposed a more plausible explanation. Subsequently elaborated by the well-known English scientist Lord Kelvin, it had the sun shrinking under the force of its own enormous gravity. As the gases compressed, they also heated up. (By then scientists were aware of the fact that compression heats a gas and expansion cools it.) Calculations showed that a shrinkage of only 200 feet a year in the sun's diameter would keep it glowing for as long as 11 million years.

The Helmholtz-Kelvin hypothesis was attractive for several reasons. It did not require any external fuel, like Mayer's meteoroids. Nor did it demand ordinary chemical reactions, such as those that occur when oil or coal burns. In fact, the idea of a gravity-fueled sun was far ahead of its time. But even in its own day, the Helmholtz-Kelvin explanation had an overwhelming drawback.

From the examination of the earth's twisting rock formations and the discovery of fossil remains of surprisingly ancient plants and animals, 19th-century geologists were already beginning to suspect that the earth was far older than a few million years. Some even thought that it was billions of years old. Obviously, if those suspicions were correct, the sun and the rest of the solar system had to be at least as old, for by then scientists were firmly agreed that the earth and other planets were born out of the sun and not vice versa. Consequently, when physicists like Lord Kelvin insisted that the earth was only a few million years old, it placed them in direct conflict with geologists.

It is one of the ironies of scientific history that the

debate was soon settled in the geologists' favor by a physicist. In 1896 the Frenchman Antoine-Henri Becquerel discovered a totally new form of energy. It was called radioactivity, and as the New-Zealand-born physicist Ernest Rutherford pointed out in a famous lecture in 1904 (which was attended by an aging and still skeptical Lord Kelvin), it made his calculations of the age of the sun totally meaningless.

Radioactivity produces heat by the spontaneous disintegration of elements like uranium. But the process is extremely slow. Rutherford and other physicists realized that it had been going on for billions of years, not just a few million. That meant that the sun, if not the earth, had to be at least as old as those radioactive materials. In addition, the discovery of radioactivity hinted at another possibility: perhaps it was the sun's mysterious energy source.

Shortly after the turn of the century, there were two other important parallel developments in physics. As a result of discoveries by Rutherford and others, scientists realized that atoms (from the Greek word for "indivisible") are not the ultimate units of matter. Instead, atoms are made up of even smaller units that seemed to be arranged like a miniature solar system. In the center of the atom was its nucleus, which consisted of particles carrying a positive electrical charge, called protons. Orbiting the nucleus were negatively charged electrons. Later, scientists discovered that the nucleus also contains particles without any charge, called neutrons.

This picture of the atom is highly simplified. Subsequently, physicists realized that the solar system model was somewhat misleading. Electrons did not really resemble orbiting planets, which occupy clearly definable places in space. Under the new quantum theory, which said energy was delivered in little packets or "quanta," matter at its most basic level had a dual nature: it could be viewed, paradoxically, as both a particle and a wave. It was as if matter had both shadow and substance. At best, the position of something as small and elusive as an electron could only be estimated at any given time or place.

The story of the atom hardly ends at this point. Since the 1930s, physicists have found that the atomic nucleus consists of dozens of baffling particles—so many, in fact, that they refer to them as their subnuclear "zoo." Lasting usually no longer than a tiny fraction of a second before they vanish from sight, most of the particles were discovered inside powerful atom smashers, or accelerators. These giant machines usually whip either electrons or protons to speeds close to that of light; then the highly energetic particles are used like bullets to batter apart the nucleus.

During such experiments, physicists confirmed a theory that seemed unbelievable when it was first put forth: every particle of matter has an equivalent particle made of a weird substance called antimatter. In effect, antimatter is a mirror image of ordinary matter. Now that the first such antimatter particles have been discovered inside accelerators, scientists have suggested that there may be vast regions out in space, perhaps even whole galaxies, made up entirely of antimatter. If such an antimatter galaxy were to bump into a galaxy made of ordinary matter, like our Milky Way, the two would totally annihilate each other in a cataclysmic explosion.

The other great development in physics following the discovery of redioactivity was the publication by Einstein in 1905 of his revolutionary papers on special relativity. In addition to explaining the nature of light, they contained the startling idea that matter and energy were interchangeable, that one was really only another form of the other. The relationship between the two was contained in the deceptively simple—and now famous—equation $e = mc^2$ (in which e stands for energy, m for mass, and c for the speed of light in a vacuum).

The implications of the equation are profound. Because c^2 (the speed of light, 186,000 miles per second, multiplied by itself) is such a large figure, even a tiny amount of matter is equivalent to an enormous amount of energy. That such a conversion could take place was shown by the phenomenon of radioactivity. As the uranium atom disintegrates, particles are released from its nucleus and from the surrounding electrons. In this breakdown process, some of the atom's mass is directly converted into energy, or heat. Exactly the same thing happens in an atomic bomb, only on a frighteningly faster and larger scale than in natural radioactive decay.

As physicists slowly began to understand Einstein's equation, they realized that the process could take place in two ways. They pointed out that energy would be released not only from the splitting—fission—of heavy atoms like uranium but also from the combining—fusion—of simple atoms like hydrogen. Indeed, much more mass is converted into energy in the fusion of hydrogen atoms than in the fission of uranium atoms. As a result, hydrogen bombs are a far more powerful weapon than atomic bombs.

As early as the 1920s, the British physicist Arthur Eddington suggested that the sun might be a great nuclear power plant. One obvious reason for such suspicions was that scientists were by then well aware of the fact that the sun was largely a great ball of very hot hydrogen. Indeed, spectral evidence had shown astronomers that hydrogen was the main ingredient of all stars like the sun. But it was not until the late 1930s that two nuclear physicists, Hans Bethe, who fled Nazi Germany for the United States, and Carl Friedrich von Weizsäcker, another German, independently explained the complicated sequence of events in the working of the thermonuclear furnaces of stars.

When temperatures deep inside the star reach some 10 million to 20 million degrees K (for the Kelvin—after Lord Kelvin—or absolute temperature scale) violent changes occur. By then the star's hydrogen atoms have been stripped of their external electrons and only nuclei consisting of a single proton remain. Stirred by the great heat, the nuclei frequently and violently bump into each other. Some of these collisions produce a new nucleus, a so-called deuteron, which consists of a proton and a neutron and is named after deuterium, a more complex form of hydrogen. The collisions also release two other particles, a positron (or positively charged electron) and a neutrino, a ghostlike particle without mass or charge that carries energy out of the star's core at the speed of light. In fact, the neutrino passes all the way through the star and out into space. The newly formed positron has a much shorter lifetime. It quickly encounters an electron. Since the two particles carry opposite charges, they immediately annihilate each other, producing still more energy.

Meanwhile, the deuteron that was formed out of the initial collision is not inactive. It meets up with a simple proton to produce a light helium nucleus, consisting of two protons and a single neutron. As in all other encounters, the violent meeting also releases energy. Finally, the newly formed helium nucleus bumps into a kindred helium nucleus. Ejecting two surplus protons, the helium nuclei form a conventional helium nucleus, consisting of two other protons and two neutrons. What happens to the two extra protons? They are returned to the star's nuclear stockpile for use in repetitions of the cycle.

This particular chain of collisions is called a proton-proton reaction, since it begins esentially with two protons. It is highly effective. Although the final product, helium, weighs only 0.71 percent less than all the fuel that has gone into the reaction, the seemingly small loss of mass in the reaction yields a significant amount of energy. (It is because the loss is so slight that the sun can keep burning for billions of years without any noticeable reduction of heat output or mass.)

In stars heavier than the sun the thermonuclear reactions are not so conservative. Their cores heat up to higher temperatures, and more violent activity ensues. The element building does not stop with the production of helium. It goes on to form still heavier elements, including carbon, nitrogen, and oxygen. In that hotter cauldron, much more energy is produced by the carbon-nitrogen-oxygen reactions than by the sun's proton-proton reactions, but they also consume far more material. That explains why stars more massive than the sun burn much more brightly and have significantly shorter lifetimes.

Understanding more about the complex events in the interior of stars is not simply a scholarly exercise for scientists. Unlike the fission reactions in conventional nuclear power plants, fusion does not produce any great amounts of dangerous radioactivity. What's more, the deuterium fuel is found in almost unlimited quantities in ordinary seawater. If scientists can duplicate the sun's thermonuclear fires on earth—as they probably will in the years ahead—mankind will have a virtually inexhaustible energy source.

4

THE BIRTH OF STARS

Imagine a Martian suddenly dropped into an earthly forest and asked to explain the life history of a tree. If the extraterrestrial visitor were shrewd enough, he would quickly realize that the unfamiliar trees grow much too slowly to reveal any secrets to him in a single afternoon's stroll. But as the canny Martian walked through the woods, he would probably see telltale signs —an acorn here, a struggling sapling there, a tree in full foilage, perhaps even an old tree trunk toppled over with age. The clever Martian would realize that he had seen trees in various stages of life. True, his visit to the forest was too brief to witness actual growth, but he probably could make some reasonably good guesses about how trees evolve.

Astronomers have used similar tactics to study the life cycles of stars. Ordinarily, the formation of stars is such a creeping process that it cannot easily be observed in an astronomer's lifetime. But by following the example of the mythical Martian, they have watched many stars in various stages of their lives.

Out of such a piecemeal approach they have been able to reconstruct the entire history of stars.

That stars have life cycles is a relatively new concept. The ancients, as noted, thought stars were fixed and permanent. But the invention of spectroscopy began to show important individual differences in stars— in temperature, brightness, size, and even chemical composition. Indeed, so much bewildering data about stars was accumulated by the new technique that two turn-of-the-century astronomers, Ejnar Hertzsprung, a Dane, and Henry Norris Russell, an American, independently devised a method for organizing the varying objects in a systematic way.

Now known as the Hertzsprung-Russell (H-R) diagram, their method involves placing stars on a graph. The vertical axis represents their absolute brightness (that is, how bright the stars are independent of their distance from us); the horizontal axis shows their surface temperature, which in turn is used to assign stars to spectral classes—B, A, F, and so on. Thus, the hottest stars are on the left side of the graph; the coolest are on the right.

As astronomers began placing stars on H-R diagrams, they found that they were not scattered helter-skelter across the chart. Surprisingly, most stars, including our sun, fell within a narrow band running from the upper left-hand corner of the diagram to the lower right. Astronomers call the band the main sequence, and it represents the place where most stars spend the greatest portion of their lives. But a star's position on the main sequence, even that of so stable a star as the sun, is not secure forever.

As a star ages and runs low on nuclear fuel, it may move off this pathway. Usually, such aging stars swell enormously in size, cool off in temperature, and change color. They may turn into what astronomers call red giants, like Betelgeuse in the constellation Orion, or even into supergiants. Such huge red or orange stars occupy places in the upper right-hand corner. Later, after they contract and heat up again, they drop to the lower left-hand corner of the diagram; the hot, luminous stars are called white dwarfs. (A typical example is the companion of Sirius.) Although the sun currently sits almost midway on the main sequence, several billion years from now it will probably balloon into a red giant, then shrink into a white dwarf.

But red giants and white dwarfs are only two of the more ordinary classes of stars. The H-R diagram is filled with more exotic stellar types, including relatively hot blue supergiants like Rigel, extremely faint stars called subdwarfs, and cool red dwarfs like nearby Barnard's star.

Ever protective of its secrets, nature creates new stars in the dense clouds of gas and dust that swirl between the stars. Consisting largely of hydrogen, the clouds tend to veil the mysterious events taking place within them. Most of this gas and dust lies in the more remote reaches of galaxies. In a spiral galaxy like the Milky Way, the clouds are mainly in the outer arms, which also happens to be where the sun is. But it is only when young stars begin to glow with their characteristic reddish light that astronomers get some inkling of the presence of stellar infants. One place relatively close to earth where the birth process is believed to be under way is in the beautifully glowing Orion nebula.

How the miraculous process begins is not entirely certain. Perhaps as the gas swirls and eddies in the cold depths of space, several smaller clouds come together. Ordinarily, the random motion of the particles making up the gases would cause them to disperse. But if enough material gathers close enough, its mutual gravitational force will build up. Like a great celestial whirlpool, the gravity field will draw in more and more dust and gas into the growing cloud. Finally, as the cloud begins to thicken and the material presses together, the gases will heat up slightly.

Even so, the cloud's fate is uncertain. Far from stable, the conglomeration of gas and dust may break up into two or more smaller clouds. Such a splitting, in fact, may be commonplace. It could account for the formation of double and triple stars, which are apparently more common than single stars like the sun. In any case, if the ball of gas reaches the right size and density, the heating will continue. Still, its temperature will be far below that needed to light any nuclear fires.

Many thousands of years may elapse before the gases have sufficiently compressed under their own weight to produce the necessary heat. Inexorably, though, contraction will continue and temperatures will climb. Finally, the temperature in the center of the cloud will have risen to about 100,000 degrees K. At this point, as has been noted, strange things begin to happen to the gas. Its atoms move about so rapidly and wildly that they knock off each other's electrons. That creates a plasma of free electrons and free protons. By now, the cloud has contracted from its original diameter of some 10 trillion miles to 100 million miles, slightly more than the distance between the sun and the earth. But even that is still too large.

Not until the cloud shrinks to only about 1 million miles, approximately the diameter of the sun, and temperatures at its core reach some 10 million to 20 million degrees K, will the nuclear fires ignite. The reason lies in one of the curiosities of nature: every proton carries a positive electrical charge, and like similar poles of a magnet they will ordinarily repel each other when they are brought together. But if protons are moving violently enough, which they do when they are heated to 10 million degrees K or more, they will smash through this electrical obstacle and approach close enough to take advantage of another of nature's basic forces: the nuclear strong force.

At work only in the very heart of the atom, this force exerts its power over a distance of less than one ten-trillionth of an inch. But once it swings into action, it will draw the once antagonistic protons together. In fact, the nuclear force is so powerful at this short range that the protons begin fusing into heavier nuclei of helium. It is at this dramatic moment that the nuclear fires are lighted, and the crucial thermonuclear reactions described in the previous chapter begin. The birth of the star can be said to have taken place.

As more and more protons fuse inside the newborn star, contraction halts. Supported by the great heat produced at its core, the star's gases resist any further tendency to collapse under their own weight. In a well-designed star like the sun, its own heat and gravity will be so carefully balanced that the star's diameter will not change appreciably for billions of years. The whole process of birth—from collapse of the cloud to nuclear ignition—may take half a million years or more. If we could watch it from afar, the cloud would seem to become increasingly luminous as it condensed into a smaller and smaller sphere. Then, as contraction ceased and thermonuclear heating took over, the star would diminish in brightness. Only in death would the star again achieve its original brilliance.

5

ENTER THE PLANETS

It was 1807 when the two professors from Connecticut
made their startling announcement. They said they had
seen rocks fall from the heavens. In the White House
then was Thomas Jefferson, perhaps the most scientifically minded of all U.S. presidents. Yet he greeted the
report with scorn. Acidly, the Virginia-born Jefferson
said that he would sooner believe that two Yankee
professors were outright liars than that stones could
tumble from the sky.

Jefferson's skepticism was hardly untypical of the
time. In Paris, members of the illustrious French
Academy also brushed off farmers who arrived with
what they said were stones from the sky. All this occurred toward the end of a period called the age of
reason. Yet unfortunately, some of the self-styled practitioners of reason could be highly unreasonable at
times, when they were confronted with new ideas. The
history of science has shown, however, that if controversial ideas are basically sound—the Copernican theory is a notable example—they will outlive their
critics.

So it has been with the stones from the sky. Since the first report of what they now call meteors (from the Greek for "things in the air"), scientists not only have come to accept them as real, but study their remnants with avid interest. Indeed, the analysis of meteorites, which are meteors that have survived the fiery passage through the earth's atmosphere, has become one of the more important adjuncts of contemporary astronomy. Such fragments are believed to trace back to the origin of the solar system. Largely unchanged since their formation, they have enabled scientists to reconstruct many of the details of that unwitnessed drama.

Dating of these interplanetary rocks indicated that the planets, including the earth, and the moon were born some 4.6 billion years ago; the date has been fully confirmed by the study of moon rocks brought home by the Apollo astronauts. This would seem to indicate that the earth's birth occurred shortly after, or perhaps even simultaneously with—scientists cannot say for sure—the birth of the sun.

The precise sequence is still not clear. A generation ago, many scientists believed in a theory proposed by two American scientists, Forest R. Moulton and Thomas C. Chamberlin, that the planets and their moons were the debris of a collision or close approach between the sun and another star. As the itinerant star passed by, its gravity tore great streamers of gas out of the sun's side. When the intruding star moved on, the material was recaptured by solar gravity and swept into great orbits around the sun. Eventually, the gases cooled, condensed, and formed the sun's family of planets.

This highly dramatic sequence is no longer generally accepted by scientists. For one thing, a stellar collision is considered very unlikely because of the wide spacing between stars. The nearest star beyond the sun, Proxima Centauri, is 24 trillion miles away. Astronomers figure that no more than ten such collisions have taken place in our part of the galaxy in the past 5 billion years. Furthermore, if the odds against stellar collisions are so high, such an explanation for the origin of the solar system would imply that planets are extremely rare.

Yet only a few years ago, the Dutch-American astronomer Peter van de Kamp of Swarthmore College's Sproul Observatory reported a strange wobble in the natural movements of nearby Barnard's star. He attributed it to the gravitational tugging of at least one planet in orbit around the star. Since then several other stars have been observed to be displaying similar wobbling, presumably also because they have planets around them. Of course, even if these planets are extremely large—comparable, say, to Jupiter—they are so distant that their faint reflected light could not be detected even in the largest earth-bound telescopes.

Rejecting the collison theory, astronomers had to look for another explanation for the birth of the planets. As it happens, a plausible theory had long been on the shelf, but periodically lost favor because of new discoveries. It was the nebular hypothesis, put forth independently by the German philosopher Immanuel Kant in 1755 and the French mathematician Pierre-Simon de Laplace in 1796. Simply stated, it says that the planets were born out of the same rotating gaseous sphere, or nebula (from the Latin word for "cloud"), as the sun.

Revived in 1945 by the physicist Carl von Weizsäcker and expanded by the Dutch-American astronomer Gerard Kuiper and others, the modern version of the old theory proposes this scenario: as the cool cloud of gas and dust contracted, it began to rotate and flatten, like twirling pizza dough. Most of the material gathered in the center at the site of the protosun, but chunks were also left out in orbit at some distance away. At first, these pieces were rather small, no bigger than baseballs. But the collisions occurred, some stuck together, held by their mutual gravitational attraction, and eventually planet-sized bodies were built up. In only one part of the solar system was the accretion process blocked. Because Jupiter's powerful gravity acted as a brake, a scattering of small particles was left strewn between the orbits of Jupiter and Mars, where otherwise a small planet might have formed. It is the asteroid belt, which is also the presumable source of most meteors.

Estimates vary on how long the process of planet formation took. Some scientists say up to 50 million years. University of Chicago chemist Edward Anders, a meteorite expert, says that the whole job could have been completed in 15 million years. Harvard astrophysicist A. G. W. Cameron thinks that it took no more than a few thousand years.

However long the birth of the planets took, the nebular theory is attractive for a number of reasons. It explains why the orbits of the planets are in the same dislike plane; the only notable exception is the orbit of the distant planet Pluto, which astronomers think may be a runaway moon of Neptune. The theory also fits in nicely with the prevailing ideas about the birth of stars, which presumably occurs at about the same time during the collapse of the rotating cloud of interstellar gases. Finally, it also accounts for the major differences that astronomers have observed in the chemistry of planets.

The giant planets Jupiter and Saturn, for instance, are largely composed of hydrogen and helium; this has been partly confirmed by the unmanned U.S. Pioneer 10 and Pioneer 11 space probes during the recent flybys of Jupiter. According to the nebular theory, these big planets were the first to be formed and hence gathered up huge amounts of raw hydrogen and helium from the original solar nebula before much chemical reaction had taken place.

In contrast, the outer planets Uranus and Neptune and probably the comets were formed after many atoms had combined into molecules. But their formation occurred in extreme conditions. Uranus and Neptune are so far from the sun that temperatures were only about a hundred degrees above absolute zero. The result was that they remained little more than a frozen mix of water, methane, and ammonia, plus a sprinkling of dust. Closer to the sun, the opposite happened: temperatures rose so high that lighter elements and compounds, including water, were mostly boiled off. Some of these gases, in fact, may have been blown clear out of the early solar system by pressure of the sun's radiation. Mainly heavier elements, such as iron, silicon, and aluminum, were left behind to provide the building blocks of the earth and other inner planets, which have approximately the same chemical composition.

The final chapter of this scenario would surely have been an awesome spectacle for any onlooker in the earth's vicinity. Already close to its full size, the earth swept up all the bits of debris still circling around it. Plunging down at speeds up to 25,000 miles per hour, they bombarded the planet in a great shower of meteors. So much heat was released upon impact that the entire surface of the young earth turned into a seething mass of glowing, molten rock. From the earth's interior, gases were released with volcanic fury to form its primitive atmosphere.

Most of the scars of this early violence have been erased by wind, rain, and the geological processes of mountain building and continental drift. But one large bit of evidence has remained. It was probably at this point in its early history that the earth acquired its moon. Some scientists think that the moon was born out of orbiting debris, like Saturn's rings. Other's argue that it was formed elsewhere in the young solar system and was captured by the earth's gravity during a close encounter. Neither argument is foolproof, and there are serious objections to each.

Other points of the primordial drama are also in dispute. Some scientists think that the global melting occurred much later in the earth's early history from the gradual buildup of heat produced by radioactive elements in the earth's outer layers. But there is no debate about the melting itself. When that happened, iron and other heavy material sank to the earth's center to form the core. Lighter material rose to create the earth's mantle and crust. On top of all this floated even less dense material, like bits of bread adrift in a thick soup, to form the continental masses.

As the earth cooled, water came bubbling out of its interior through volcanoes and other cracks. Collecting in the large basins between the continents, it formed the oceans. Gradually the earth began to take on its familiar appearance. The stage was also set for the next great event in the earth's history: the start of the complex sequence of chemical steps leading up to the formation of the first primitive, one-celled forms of life in the young planet's seas.

6

NEW WINDOW
ON THE UNIVERSE

Erected in the midst of an abandoned potato field outside the small town of Holmdel, New Jersey, in the
year 1931, the large contraption looked strange indeed. Resembling the wire-and-strut wings of a World
War I biplane, the oddly shaped machine stretched
100 feet from end to end. It was set on four wheels
that had been taken from an abandoned Model T
Ford, was placed over a circular track, and could
swing completely around like a carousel.

Playful as the carousel may have seemed, its builder,
a twenty-three-year-old radio engineer at the Bell
Telephone Laboratories named Karl Jansky, had a
very serious purpose in mind. The device was a large,
rotating antenna, one of the first instruments of its
kind. He had designed and constructed it for some
scientific detective work. He wanted to track down
the source of inexplicable crackling noises that were
interfering with radio transmissions to ships at sea and
across the Atlantic.

As often happens in science, Jansky discovered

something completely unexpected. As the antenna made a complete sweep of the skies every 20 minutes, he picked up static from all directions. Some of the radio noise was quickly traced; it was created in the electrical activity of squalls and thunderstorms. But he also detected a weaker hisslike noise that left him baffled. Rising in the east and setting in the west like the sun, it seemed to be coming from a different part of the sky at different hours of the day.

Most technicians probably would not have spent much time fretting over the peculiar hissing. It was so faint it hardly seemed of any consequence. But Jansky would not let the puzzle rest. A frail, dedicated young man who suffered from a chronic kidney disease, he examined every conceivable cause—flaws in the antenna, disturbances by nearby power lines, electrical storms, stray signals from radio transmitters in the vicinity. Nothing seemed to explain the noise.

For a time, the strongest signals came from the direction of the sun. But, strangely, they soon began drifting away from the sun by a small amount each day. It was then that Jansky picked up a significant clue. After carefully timing the appearance of the strongest signals each day over a period of several months, he realized that they were coming four minutes earlier every night. Consulting an astronomy textbook, he quickly confirmed his suspicions. As the earth moves in its orbit around the sun, a slightly different portion of the sky comes into view every night, and the same stars rise over the horizon four minutes earlier every night. The effect is called sidereal (or star) time, as opposed to ordinary time derived from the earth's movements with respect to the sun.

For Jansky, the time lag of the hiss was now understandable. The signals did not originate in the earth's vicinity. Nor did they come from the sun. Their source was the stars. The ancients had spoken poetically of the music of the spheres. Now, using the most modern of listening devices, Jansky had finally heard this celestial song.

Continuing his investigations, he managed to narrow down the source of his "star noise" to the constellation Sagittarius, the archer, a grouping of stars identified by the ancients as a centaur, a fabled creature that was half man and half horse and was shooting an arrow. Only a few years before Jansky's investigations, astronomers had realized that the region, packed with stars and gases, was actually the center of the Milky Way galaxy. That means Jansky was apparently picking up faint radio whispers from more than 26,-000 light-years away.

Jansky's accidental discovery opened up a completely new window on the universe. Until then, astronomers could only view the skies in "visible light." Although telescopes and other optical gadgetry have vastly improved the human eye's performance, its capabilities are extremely limited. Through millions of years of evolution, our eyes have learned to respond only to a small portion of what scientists call the electromagnetic spectrum. Even with the best telescopes, we are blind to other parts of the spectrum. It is as if we could see only objects of one color—say, the green leaves of trees—yet remained oblivious to the majestic blue of the sky and sea or the dark browns and purples of distant landscapes.

That other types of light exist, apart from the light visible to our eyes, did not become apparent to scientists until the astronomer William Herschel performed a Newton-type experiment with a prism around 1800. Placing a thermometer just beyond the red end of the sun's spectrum, he noticed that the instrument was heating up, although no light seemed to be shining on it. Obviously, something had to be providing the heat. Scientists called the invisible radiation infrared, or beyond red, from its position in the spectrum.

Largely because of the pioneering work of the 19th-century Scottish physicist James Clerk Maxwell, it is now known that infrared light is only another slice of the electromagnetic spectrum, which consists of a variety of waves, all traveling at the familiar speed of visible light. The only basic difference in the waves is their length or frequency. (These two characteristics have an inverse relationship: the longer the wavelength, the lower the frequency—that is, the number of waves traveling past a given point in a given period of time.) The shortest of all electromagnetic waves are the gamma rays; these measure less than a trillionth of an inch from the crest of one wave to the next. Following in order of increasing length are X rays, ultraviolet rays, the colors of the visible spectrum, infrared waves, and radio waves. The last are the longest, measuring from a fraction of an inch (in the case of microwaves) to as long as several miles.

For astronomers, radio waves have a special usefulness. Except for visible light and a small portion of the infrared and ultraviolet spectrum, they are the only form of radiation that easily penetrates the atmosphere. Ultraviolet rays, X rays, and gamma rays are largely screened off by this protective blanket. If they were not, the inhabitants of the earth would be seriously imperiled by the lethal radiation.

Actually, the atmosphere also blocks most longer radio wavelengths. Only very short radio waves manage to reach the ground. But even these limited frequencies are extremely important, for they let astronomers see the heavens in a totally new light that was previously totally hidden from them.

At first, astronomers were slow to appreciate the full value of Jansky's discovery. That was not surprising. All too often scientists tend to ignore the work of people outside their specialties. Moreover, earlier attempts to detect signals from the skies had failed completely. In the 1890s, shortly after the discovery of radio waves, the British physicist Oliver Lodge tried to pick up radio signals from the sun, but decided that they could never be heard because of strong electromagnetic disturbances on earth.

Jansky himself did not pursue his investigations of star noise for long, since neither he nor his superiors at Bell Labs saw its potential scientific value. For a while he considered teaching at the State University of Iowa. But he chose instead to remain in Holmdel, where he became Bell Labs' chief "noise" expert, always consulted when serious static problems turned up in radio transmissions. During World War II, he applied some of the knowledge that he had acquired in building directional antennas for his sky search to designate radio direction finders. These were used, not only as navigational tools, but to help locate enemy radio stations.

Radio astronomy began in earnest after the war when radio engineers and physicists who had worked on radar turned their talents to building similar antennas to listen to the skies. Jansky, however, saw only the first tentative beginnings of the science he had founded. His kidney ailment steadily worsening, he had to limit his activities. In 1950 he died of a stroke at the age of 44.

Fortunately for the young science, Jansky's original work had been quickly followed up by an enthusiastic young radio "ham" in Illinois. Like Jansky, Grote Reber was not trained in astronomy, but he had been interested in radio since he was a teenager. In 1927, when he was only 15 years old, he had already built a shortwave radio transmitter and was exchanging messages with other hams round the world. A few years later, when he heard of Jansky's discovery, he decided to listen to star noise.

Working alone, he built a 31-foot "pie plate" antenna in his backyard in Wheaton, Illinois, at a cost of $2000 (no small sum for a young man in the depth of the depression!). Resting on a wooden framework, the dish could be tilted toward different parts of the sky. In his basement, he rigged up a simple recording device; any signals captured by the antenna would be registered by movements of a small needle.

Reber was so anxious to begin radio observing that he could barely wait to get home from his job with a radio company in Chicago, 30 miles away, at the end of each working day and begin his long nightly vigils.

Now you can own it all. Everything Shakespeare ever wrote. Every comedy. Every tragedy. Every historical drama. Every epic and romantic poem. Every finely-chiseled sonnet.

They're yours in three handsome volumes for only $1, as your introduction to The Classics Club.

The Classics Club is quite unlike any other book club. It doesn't offer best sellers that come and go. Instead, it offers its members a chance to stay young through great books that will never grow old.

These books include Utopia by Thomas More; the wisdom of Plato, Aristotle, and Marcus Aurelius; Benjamin Franklin's Autobiography; Omar Khay-

(Continued on other side)

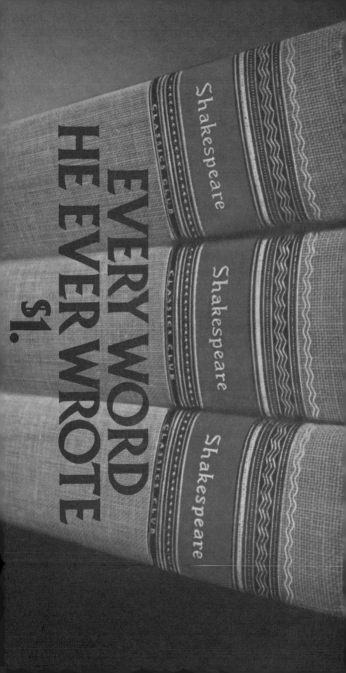

EVERY WORD
HE EVER WROTE

$1.

Shakespeare

Shakespeare

Shakespeare

At first, he was disappointed; apparently tuned to the wrong wavelengths, the antenna did not pick up anything interesting. Then, late one night in October 1938, the needle began to jiggle. He was finally receiving Jansky's star noise.

Reber not only confirmed the original signals from Sagittarius, but found other "radio stars." One particularly strong one was in the constellation Cygnus (the swan); another in Canis Major (the larger dog). Strong noises also originated in Cassiopeia (the mother of Andromeda). Curiously, the signals often came from regions of the sky where no stars were visible. This suggested something sensational: that there might be objects in the sky that give off significant amounts of energy other than visible light.

These discoveries attracted a certain amount of interest, as did the original design of Reber's antenna which was the world's first "dish" radio telescope. But Reber nonetheless found it difficult to raise money for his experiments. On one occasion, he was helped by a fluke of the weather. A research foundation's grant committee had come to inspect his observatory. But it was overcast and rainy. The committee decided to leave, since it assumed that radio astronomy, like visible light observing, needed clear skies. Making the most of the opportunity, Reber showed the visitors that he could observe even on such a bad day. The committee was so impressed it approved a grant for his work.

Though scientific research in the U.S. and Europe was soon directed almost entirely toward the war effort, radio astronomy profited indirectly from a wartime discovery. In 1942, at the height of the fighting, British radar experts inadvertently picked up extremely short microwave bursts from the sun. It was not an especially welcome discovery. The sun's radio waves severely interfered with the attempts to track enemy rockets and planes, and the British kept the solar emissions a highly guarded secret. But it marked one of the first milestones in the emergence of radio astronomy.

Following up their interest in the sun during peacetime, British scientists linked the periodic radio outbursts with sunspots, which are relatively dark (or cool) regions on the solar surface that are the center of great magnetic storms. Jansky had apparently failed to detect these noises because he worked during a period of minimal sunspot activity. Such observations, in any case, required new and larger radio telescopes. The design of these instruments was pioneered mainly by British, Australian, and Dutch scientists, many of whom had acquired their experience during the war in working with radar.

The new telescopes took a variety of forms. Easily the most common type was the large dish, or paraboloid, like Reber's original backyard pie-plate antenna in Wheaton. Like the mirrors of optical telescopes, such dishes collect electromagnetic energy in this case radio waves—and focus it on a smaller antenna in front of the paraboloid. From this collector, the signals are piped into a control center, where they are processed and amplified. Fed into ordinary loudspeakers, they emerge as a weird mix of beeps, squawks, and hums that sounds like electronic music. More commonly, the signals are traced out by a stylus on a moving roll of graph paper. They may also be stored on magnetic tape for analysis by computer.

Because radio waves are some 100,000 times longer than light waves, radio astronomers need bigger "lenses" to trap them. For a long time, the largest fully steerable dish antenna was the Jodrell Bank telescope in Britain. Built under the leadership of Sir Bernard Lovell, it has a diameter of 250 feet. More recently, a 330-foot fully steerable reflector was erected near Bonn in West Germany. Even though such telescopes can "see" farther than their optical counterparts, they cannot see as sharply. That is, they have less resolving power, or ability to distinguish two objects that are close to each other. For example, a single dish would have to be more than 300 miles in diameter to achieve a resolving power at radio frequencies comparable to the 200-inch telescope in visible light.

Radio astronomers operate under other handicaps. Unlike their optical colleagues, who must wait for clear, still nights, they can listen to the signals from deep space in almost any weather, except electrical storms. But they must always be on guard against local electronic interference. For instance, when Jodrell Bank first searched for pulsars, it mistakenly tuned in to the buzzes of electrical fences around nearby cow pastures. Airport radar beacons have also played havoc with the efforts of radio astronomers—as have such common kinds of electronic pollution as faulty automobile ignition systems, strong radio stations, and hospital diathermy machines. Lately, radio astronomers have even been complaining about interference from the powerful signals of orbiting satellites. Almost any extraneous noise means trouble for radio astronomers. Even though the signals they are trying to listen to are created by unimaginably violent events—the explosion of stars, the spin of a pulsar, or the upheaval of a galaxy—the energy received on earth is usually only a faint whisper. The Crab nebula, for instance, is one of the "brightest" radio sources in the sky, yet it covers the entire earth with no more than 100 watts of electrical power, just enough to light an ordinary bulb. Quasars are perhaps the most distant objects in the universe; their powerful signals produce less than a watt of power by the time they reach us. Explaining the fragile nature of the signals they work with, radio astronomers point out that the total energy collected by all their telescopes in the first two decades of radio astronomy amounted to no more than that of a single snowflake hitting the ground.

To cope with these difficulties, radio astronomers have built increasingly larger telescopes. At Green Bank, West Virginia, the National Radio Astronomy Observatory operates a partly steerable dish almost as big as the giant Bonn antenna. In Arecibo, Puerto Rico, there is an even bigger telescope carved out of a natural limestone valley. Carefully contoured and covered with wire mesh, the dish is 1000 feet across and has a collecting area of 20 acres, more than that of all the radio and optical telescopes ever built. Suspended by cables some fifty stories above its surface is a smaller, movable collecting antenna. By maneuvering the device, the Arecibo astronomers can scan up to 40 percent of the sky at any one time. The earth's daily rotation provides additional coverage. (The giant dish can also act as a radar beacon, sending out signals as well as receiving them.)

Despite its great size, the Arecibo instrument has neither the resolution nor the sensitivity of the largest "light buckets," as optical astronomers call their instruments. Objects must be at least a sixth of a degree apart, or about the width of the quarter moon, for the dish to distinguish them. To match the performance of the big mirrors, radio astronomers at Arecibo and elsewhere use an ingenious stratagem. By aiming two telescopes at the same object they achieve results comparable to those produced by a single antenna with a diameter as large as the distance between them.

The tactic works because of the basic wave nature of radio signals. If they happen to be coming from a radio source directly above a spot midway between the two telescopes, the same waves will arrive at each antenna at exactly the same time. The signals will be "in phase," as scientists say; that is, when the peak or valley of a wave crosses one antenna the same peak or valley will be crossing the other. The result is a signal twice as strong as one that can be obtained with only a single telescope. This lets radio astronomers hear faint signals that might otherwise be inaudible.

When the object's position changes, however, the signals will arrive at each telescope at slightly different times. The peak of one wave may strike one dish just as its valley is reaching the other. When that happens, the waves tend to weaken or "interfere" with each other. In fact, the radio source may be so positioned above the telescopes that its waves almost completely cancel each other out. But such effects can be highly desirable. Astronomers can use them to tell, for example, how wide a radio source is, and even whether it consists of two separate sources.

Imagine that the radio telescopes are two television cameras photographing the same object—say, a cube —against a darkened background. If the cameras are close together, they will produce almost identical pictures of the cube; the engineers in the studio can then easily overlay the two pictures electronically to produce a single clear image of the cube. But as the cameras are separated, they will see the cube from noticeably different angles. No longer will the engineers be able to combine the pictures into a single cube without blurring. The point where such confusion in the images begins depends on the size of the cube. The larger it is, the sooner differences show up as the cameras move apart. If the engineers want to know how large the cube is, they can watch for the onset of blurring. Similarly, radio astronomers can gauge the size of a radio object in the sky by watching for the start of confusion in its radio waves.

In recent years radio astronomers have been using telescopes increasingly farther apart, often separated by entire continents. Such long baselines give the telescopes a diameter almost as large as the earth. The technique, known as very-long baseline interferometry, was pioneered by Canadian radio astronomers, who matched up the 150-foot dish of the Algonquin Radio Observatory in Ontario with a similar dish across Canada in British Columbia. Since then such linkups have multiplied. The Algonquin telescope has been paired with Jodrell Bank; it has also been connected with the Parkes telescope in Australia. Arecibo, in turn, has joined forces with an antenna in Sweden. Hookups have been made between telescopes in the U.S. and the Soviet Union. But the irrepressible radio astronomers hope for still longer baselines—perhaps between an observatory on earth and an orbiting satellite or a future telescope on the moon.

In the earliest experiments of this kind the telescopes were linked by radio; the signals received at one antenna were compared with those at the other by transmitting them between telescopes. But the timing in such experiments is so critical that as the baselines became longer, even the passage of the radio waves from one telescope to the other introduced errors. Now, in very-long-baseline interferometry, astronomers no longer use radio connections between the receiving sites. Instead, the signals are recorded at each telescope on magnetic tape. At regular intervals, extremely precise timing beeps from atomic clocks are added to the tape. Later the recorded signals from each telescope are brought together and matched by computer. The computer works with such accuracy that the final "picture" is almost as accurate as if the two telescopes had been miraculously connected by some instantaneous signaling system.

Radio astronomers use still another technique to get clear radio pictures. Largely developed by Sir Martin Ryle of Britain's Mullard Radio Astronomy Observatory at Cambridge University, it uses several smaller telescopes that can be moved over a fixed area. As they are maneuvered about, all the while scanning the same radio object, they gradually accumulate the signals that would have been picked up by one telescope as big as the whole area. The method is called aperture synthesis, since it synthesizes, or artificially duplicates, the performance of a telescope of much larger aperture, or diameter.

In 1972, the British observatory completed its "Five-Kilometer" telescope under the direction of Ryle, who has since been awarded a Nobel prize for his work. Not a single telescope in the usual sense, the instrument is an array consisting of eight 42-foot dishes, spread out along an east-west line of nearly 5 kilometers (3 miles). Four of the telescopes are fixed in place; the other four can be moved along an abandoned railroad track which was once part of the line that linked Cambridge with Oxford. By such maneuvering, Ryle obtains pictures of radio objects comparable to those that would be produced by a 5-kilometer-wide antenna.

The technique has been widely used. Near Canberra, Australia, for example, radio astronomer Bernard Mills has laid out two lines of antennas in the shape of an X that spreads over a quarter of a mile of grazing land. Instruments similar to the Mills cross have been built in the U.S., the Netherlands, Canada, and the Soviet Union; radio astronomers sometimes jokingly call the Russian telescope the red cross.

But even the largest of these instruments will eventually be eclipsed by a giant telescope under construction near Socorro, New Mexico. The so-called Very Large Array (VLA) will consist of 27 separate 85-foot antennas spread over 26 miles of desert in the shape of a huge Y; all the telescopes will be maneuverable on carefully laid out railroad tracks. When the monstrous instrument is completed in the early 1980s, radio astronomers expect to get pictures almost as sharply focused as those produced by the largest optical telescopes. From their desert site, they should be able to peer into the heart of the most distant radio galaxies and perhaps even into the enigmatic quasars.

7

THE SONG
OF HYDROGEN

People often talk of the vast, empty reaches of space. But strictly speaking, space is far from empty. There are, of course, regions between the stars so devoid of matter that they form a far better vacuum than can be produced in any earthly laboratory. Still, even these regions are sprinkled with stray bits of matter; they are spread so thin that if scientists could isolate a pint of the stuff, they might not find more than a single atom, compared with hundreds of millions of atoms that would still be left in a like-sized container emptied by the best pump on earth. The universe is so large, however, that if the material between the stars could be piled up, it might well outweigh all of them.

Most of this interstellar material consists of great clouds of hydrogen, the simplest and most common element and also the basic building block of stars. Although astronomers have long yearned to study the hydrogen clouds, they found them elusive. Extremely cold and carrying no electrical charge, the clouds give off no visible radiation. Thus they could not readily be examined—at least not until an unusual discovery by a young Dutch astronomer, Hendrik van de Hulst, in 1944 during World War II.

Working under the oppressive conditions of the Nazi occupation of his country, van de Hulst, then 25, did ingenious mathematical calculations showing that the hydrogen atom can sometimes act like a very weak radio transmitter. Under ordinary circumstances, the hydrogen atom consists of a single proton circled by a single electron, with both spinning, like tops, in the same direction. But for reasons still not clear, the electron occasionally flips over, spinning in a different direction from the proton. In that brief instant, the atom gives off a tiny pulse of radio energy. Its wavelength is about 21 centimeters (8.4 inches), or roughly in the range of radar or other microwave signals.

Van de Hulst figured that any single atom of hydrogen was unlikely to flip over more than once in 11 million years. Yet there are so many free-floating hydrogen atoms in space that there would be a steady 21-centimeter hum from all their flip-flops. In fact, he speculated, the radiation should be strong enough to be detected on earth. But in wartime Holland he had no way to check his prediction.

In 1951, at the suggestion of the Harvard physicist Edward Purcell, a graduate physics student at Harvard named Harold Ewen set about building a receiver that could detect "the song of hydrogen." His "ear" was a small, pyramid-shaped horn antenna specifically designed to pick up 21-centimeter radio waves. Poking out of a window in a Harvard physics building in the dead of winter, the antenna was a favorite target of snowball-throwing students. But fortunately the bombardment caused more annoyance than damage. When the first faint signals came trickling in, Purcell could hardly believe what he heard. He checked immediately with radar experts in the Boston area to make sure their transmitters were not causing the noise. Only when Purcell was finally convinced that they were not some terrestrial phenomenon did he announce the detection of signals from the great hydrogen clouds out in space.

Van de Hulst's colleagues in Holland might have beaten the Americans to the discovery, but a fire had temporarily knocked out their equipment. Back in operation a few weeks later, the Dutch radio astronomers soon confirmed the discovery, as did scientists in Australia. The great international interest underscored the importance of the detection of 21-centimeter radiation. Except perhaps for the accidental reception of radio waves from the sun in the midst of the war, the discovery marked the greatest advance in radio astronomy since the pioneering days of Jansky and Reber. Some optical astronomers had still doubted the usefulness of "listening" to the heavens rather than looking at them, but the signals from the invisible hydrogen clouds convinced them that radio astronomy had an extremely important contribution to make. As a new science it had come of age.

Radio astronomers soon made good use of the song of hydrogen. Positioned as we are in the vicinity of a star at the edge of the galactic disk, astronomers must look toward the galaxy's center to unravel the details of its structure. Here, ordinary telescopes are of little help. Great clouds of dust almost totally blot out the light from that portion of the sky. The dust, however, is no obstacle to 21-centimeter waves, which easily pass through the interstellar debris. Van de Hulst and other radio astronomers at Holland's Leiden Observatory quickly seized the opportunity to map the shape of the galaxy.

As their surveying tool they used a radio telescope made mostly from the remains of an old German radar antenna left rusting on a beach after the war. Pointing the telescope toward the center of the galaxy, they picked up strong hydrogen emissions. These did not let them see individual stars, but helped them do the next best thing: to trace the outlines of the large hydrogen clouds in which the stars are found. Slowly scanning the sky, the radio astronomers eventually gathered enough information about the distribution of these clouds to provide graphic confirmation of what the American astronomer Harlow Shapley and other optical observers had begun to suspect back in the 1920s: that the Milky Way is a great spiral of stars whose arms swirl out from the center like the design on a whirling mechanical sparkler. The Dutch astronomers, led by Jan Oort, also discovered that the entire galaxy is surrounded by a thin halo of hydrogen. Subsequently, as other radio observers began listening to the song of hydrogen, they found similar radio halos around other spiral galaxies, including the neighboring galaxy in Andromeda, M31 (so named because it is the 31st object in a catalogue of nebulas started by the 18th-century French astronomer Charles Messier).

The interest of radio astronomers was not limited to hydrogen clouds. As the number of new radio ears increased, many of them were put to work looking for "discrete radio sources." Hydrogen clouds are usually spread over wide areas, but discrete sources seem to occupy only a very small portion of the sky. Reber had originally called such sources radio stars, but in general they are not stars. Most stars are far too distant for their weak radio signals to be heard. An exception is the sun, whose static was so disturbing to British radar experts during World War II. Usually the sun's radio emissions are very faint, but in its more tempestuous moments the sun can indirectly create so much noise that radio communications on earth are seriously affected.

Fortunately for terrestrial communications, most of the sun's output consists of thermal (heat) radiation. As its name suggests, thermal radiation is produced by very hot, glowing objects, like molten iron in a furnace. Futhermore, as their temperature increases, they give off radiation of shorter and shorter wavelengths. Radio waves, on the other hand, are even longer than the longest visible red light waves. Thus, even though they are very bright, hot objects like iron in a furnace

—or the sun—tend to give off very little radio energy compared to their visible light.

When the sun does occasionally produce brief bursts of extremely powerful radio waves, they are generated by nonthermal means linked to sunspots. Observed by Chinese astronomers more than 2000 years ago, these small dark patches remained largely a mystery until they were studied early in this century by the American astronomer George Ellery Hale, who founded the great astronomical observatories atop California's Mount Wilson and Palomar that now bear his name. It was Hale who determined that sunspot regions are, besides being cooler than the rest of the sun's surface, the center of very strong magnetic fields.

Largely cyclical, the formation of sunspots reaches a peak about once every 11 years. Furthermore, sunspots usually occur in pairs with magnetic fields of opposite polarity. If compasses could be put in the vicinity of two neighboring sunspots, the needles would point in exactly reversed directions. At the height of the sunspot cycle the magnetic fields often become so unstable that they apparently cause violent electrical discharges like great bolts of lightning.

Such eruptions appear as very bright areas above the sun's surface called solar flares, which release a barrage of charged particles—mostly electrons and protons—known as cosmic rays. As the particles are whipped to enormous energies (or speeds) by the strong magnetic fields, they produce intense electromagnetic radiation, including X rays and radio waves. The phenomenon is quite similar to what occurs on a smaller scale when nuclear physicists speed up particles by powerful magnetic fields inside circular atom smashers, or accelerators, called synchrotrons. Hence the radiation produced by these giant man-made machines as well as that of the sun's magnetic storms is called synchrotron radiation.

The sun is not the only source of such radiation in the solar system. The giant planet Jupiter gives off a continuous stream of radio waves. After these powerful Jovian crackling noises were discovered in 1955 by the Americans Bernard Burke and Kenneth Franklin, some astronomers speculated that they might be caused by the planet's great red spot or thunderstorms in its atmosphere. But the successive flybys of the planet in 1973 and 1974 by Pioneer 10 and Pioneer 11 convinced scientists that much of the Jovian static has a different origin. The robot spacecraft radioed back data indicating that large numbers of charged particles are trapped in Jupiter's magnetic fields. Periodically distorted by the inner Jovian moon Io, these changing fields accelerate the particles to tremendous velocities. As in the sun's magnetic storms, the result is synchrotron radiation. The ringed planet Saturn, which resembles Jupiter in many ways, is also thought to be producing such radiation.

As celestial radio transmitters go, however, neither the sun nor any of its satellites is exceptional. As they listened to the heavens, radio astronomers located thousands of other radio sources that give off radio energy at rates millions of times greater. Only their enormous distance from earth makes their output seem no louder than a whisper, just as the brightest stars appear dim in optical telescopes if they are far enough away. One of the strongest sources beyond the solar system lies in the constellation Taurus. Because it was the first to be discovered there radio astronomers call it Taurus A; in fact, it was while Jupiter was passing nearby that its radiation was accidentally detected. What made the discovery of Taurus A so exceptional was not only its strength as a radio beacon; its study marked the beginning of an important partnership between radio and optical astronomy.

Once radio astronomers had determined Taurus A's location, optical astronomers had no difficulty finding an object in their telescopes. The powerful radio transmitter turned out to be the familiar Crab nebula. Located some 6500 light-years away, it is one of the most extraordinary sights in the sky, a great expanding cloud of gases that got its name from the 19th-century Irish astronomer the Earl of Rosse, who thought it looked like a crab. The gases are still expanding at velocities of more than 60 million miles per day.

Almost immediately after they linked Taurus A to the Crab, scientists thought the radio emissions were the result of synchrotron radiation. But they had no way to prove their suspicions until the Russian astrophysicist Iosef S. Shklovskii proposed a simple test. If the radiation was the product of great magnetic fields, he said, they should also be disturbing the Crab's visible light in a predictable way: the light waves should be polarized, or more or less aligned in a single plane, like a rope wiggling only up and down rather than in all directions. Astronomers quickly set about examining the nebula's light in a polarizing filter, which blocks out all light except the waves moving in the direction for which the device has been set. Just as Shklovskii had predicted, the Crab nebula's light was heavily polarized. For the scientists, the implications of these observations were clear: the beautifully multicolored cloud—or perhaps something in its midst —was behaving like an enormously powerful cosmic particle accelerator.

Since then radio astronomers have found that most other radio sources can also be explained best by syncthrotron radiation. That means there are magnetic fields everywhere in the heavens whirling charged particles around with incredible energy. The only apparent exceptions are areas like the Orion nebula, whose radio emissions seem to be of thermal origin. Unlike the Crab, the Orion nebula is a region where gases are condensing into new stars. As they are formed, they heat up enormously and glow brightly. But their output of radio energy never reaches the levels of synchrotron radiation.

Easily the strongest of the new radio sources was found in the W-shaped constellation Cassiopeia, which radio astronomers have nicknamed "Cass." Noisier than even the Crab, Cass A also more elusive. Even after they had gotten the general location of the source from their radio counterparts, optical astronomers had considerable difficulty finding any visible object at the site.

It was only after the 200-inch Palomar telescope was mobilized for the search that astronomers zeroed in on the apparent target: another region of expanding gases more than 11,000 light-years away. The hunt for the radio source's visible light image was not just an exercise in scientific curiosity. By themselves radio telescopes cannot usually be used to gauge a radio source's distance. For this its visible counterpart must be found and optical measures used.

About this time, radio astronomers realized that radio emissions were also coming from clouds in the constellations Gemini, the twins, and Auriga, the charioteer. But they could not be sure whether the gases of these clouds are expanding like the Crab's or whether they are coming together to form new stars, as in the Orion nebula. Of one thing they were certain, however: the clouds were only an astronomical stone's throw away, whereas the vast majority of radio sources turned out to be separate galaxies far beyond the Milky Way.

All this was surprising to astronomers. Most spiral galaxies are very weak emitters of radio energy. A typical spiral like the Milky Way radiates about a million times more energy in light than radio waves. But in radio galaxies the energy output is reversed: they are producing radio waves at levels up to a million times higher than their light waves. What is causing this topsy-turvy situation? Again, the answer came out of the new, highly productive collaboration of radio and optical astronomy.

When the German astronomer Walter Baade finally managed to track down the optical counterpart of a powerful extragalactic radio source called Cygnus A with the Palomar 200-inch mirror, he could scarcely believe what he saw on his photographic plates. At the source's apparent site in the constellation Cygnus, the Swan, he found not one but two galaxies; they were either colliding—or ripping apart. Learning of Baade's incredible pictures, radio astronomers turned their telescopes back to Cygnus A. The reexamination confirmed Baade's finding: the signals from Cygnus A were made up of several sources. Two of the sources seemed to be located in the very heart of the extragalactic upheaval visible in Baade's plates, while two others came from regions out in space, apparently beyond the galaxies. However these findings were interpreted, either as colliding galaxies or galaxies splitting apart, astronomers agreed that Cygnus A was the setting of an extremely violent cosmic upheaval unlike any seen before.

The discovery of other examples of such extragalactic turmoil quickly followed. In the southern constellation Centaurus, optical astronomers found that a multiple radio source was another suspected case of two galaxies in collision. Known to optical astronomers as NGC5128 (for New General Catalogue, after a listing of celestial objects made by the 19th-century Danish astronomer J. L. E. Dreyer), it appears on photographic plates as a bright, glowing region split in the middle by a dark band. (We now know that NGC5128 is a single galaxy undergoing an explosion.) From another tip by radio astronomers, optical astronomers spotted signs of a similar cataclysm in the Perseus cluster of galaxies, of which either two were crashing or one was being ripped apart. Before radio astronomers began picking up strong noises from it, optical astronomers had paid little heed to a bright elliptical galaxy in the constellation Virgo called M87. Then they decided to take a more careful look. By cutting down the length of time they exposed their photographic plates to M87's light, they were able to bring out details in the galaxy's core that were previously washed out. Astonishingly, a bright blue jet of gases was streaming out of the core, as if propelled by a mightly explosion or tidal force.

Another galactic eruption came to light after radio astronomers heard noises from M82, an irregular galaxy in the constellation Ursa Major, the Big Bear, which includes the stars that form the Big Dipper. Carefully clocking the velocity of the galaxy's exploding gases, Palomar astronomers Allan Sandage and C. Roger Lynds determined that they were moving off into space at 620 miles per second. Even more violent events seem to be going on inside the extremely bright centers of another class of galaxies discovered by the Harvard astronomer Carl Seyfert. Now named after him, Seyfert galaxies give off both visible and radio energy in doses far exceeding what one would expect from their very compact size.

These findings raised profound new questions for astronomers. Why were certain galaxies giving off energy at such prodigious rates? Why was material being ejected so violently from them? The collision of galaxies could account for some of these mind-boggling observations, but certainly not all of them, since the statistical chances of many such smashups were not high even in a universe of millions upon millions of galaxies. More important, in some cases the energy output is so huge that even an event as cataclysmic as the collision of two galaxies could not ordinarily account for it, unless the galaxies totally annihilated each other.

In barely fifteen years since the birth of their science at the end of World War II, radio astronomers had opened up a whole new universe. It was unimaginably vast and violent. It also posed new problems for scientists to solve. But even as they grappled with these puzzles, more discoveries were made, complicating their task.

8

MOLECULES
BETWEEN THE STARS

Almost as if it came out of nowhere, the large dark cloud suddenly bore down on the solar system. Scientists on earth could only watch helplessly as it rapidly approached. Positioning itself between the earth and the sun, the cloud seemed to be trying to rejuvenate itself in the warmth of the solar thermonuclear fires. The cloud was so large that it periodically blocked off almost all the earth's sunlight, sending frozen shivers across the planet.

It did not take scientists long to realize that the intruder was not simply a collection of dirt and cosmic debris, but composed of extremely complex molecules. The cloud's chemistry was, in fact, so evolved that the great mass in the sky was actually alive and had an intelligence far greater than that of any earthlings. Through an elaborate system of signals the earth's scientists tried to persuade the cloud to leave. But the politicians would have none of it; instead of negotiating, they fired hydrogen bombs at the cloud, which it simply deflected back to the earth, causing general havoc.

Finally, almost as suddenly and as mysteriously as it came, the dark blot drifted back into the depths of space, leaving behind a battered but highly relieved earth.

This succession of events never occurred, of course, except in the lively mind of Britain's Sir Fred Hoyle, who is not only an eminent astronomer but a first-rate science fiction writer. In his book *The Black Cloud,* he described the invasion of the solar system by a super-intelligent blob of matter. But as farfetched as his story may seem, it has unexpectedly turned out to have some basis in fact. Since Hoyle wrote his book in the 1950s, radio astronomers have learned that complex chemical reactions can indeed occur in the great clouds of matter between the stars. Not only do their atoms combine into simple molecules, but these in turn link up into more complex molecules.

The fact that chemistry can take place in open space took astronomers by surprise. For a long time they were convinced that the expanses between the stars were entirely empty. When William Herschel first spotted dark interstellar clouds two centuries ago, he quite seriously explained to his sister Caroline, who was also his assistant, that these were "holes in the sky" through which astronomers could look out toward infinity.

By the beginning of the 20th century astronomers had identified a few free-floating atoms in space during spectroscopic studies. But it hardly seemed possible to them that conditions in space would permit these atoms to react with each other. Temperatures in interstellar regions were very low, only a few degrees above absolute zero. Individual atoms were so widely scattered that the statistical chances of many meetings were impossibly small. And even if some atoms managed to link up, it seemed likely that their bonds would quickly be broken by the harsh glare of ultraviolet radiation from nearby stars or the bombardment of cosmic rays.

In the 1930s optical astronomers provided the first hints that such suppositions could be wrong. As noted earlier, when light from a star passes through gases on its way to the earth, it is affected in a curious way: at certain places in its spectrum, dark lines, or absorption bands, appear. These represent light that has been absorbed by the gases lying between the star and the earth. Furthermore, since they are always characteristic of the gas that created them, the lines can be used like fingerprints to identify the gases.

Among the early molecules detected by such spectral fingerprinting were carbon monoxide (CO) and titanium monoxide (TiO), which were located in the relatively cool outer atmospheres of red giants like Betelgeuse. Astronomers also found several free radicals, or fragments of molecules, in the clouds between the stars. A typical example is the free radical cyanogen (CN), which consists of a single atom of carbon and one of nitrogen. But this was about as far as ordinary optical spectroscopy could take astronomers. More detailed studies were impossible because some of the best hunting grounds for molecules in space are obscured behind large dust clouds, which block off visible light. (It is the dust, incidentally, that apparently provides shielding for the molecules, protecting them from destructive radiation.)

Radio astronomers soon realized that they might be able to peer behind these dark barriers. Unlike shorter light waves, the 21-centimeter emissions from hydrogen easily pass through the dust. One of the first scientists to suggest the use of radio techniques to hunt for interstellar molecules was the American physicist Charles H. Townes, who shared a Nobel prize for his work on the principle of the laser, which gives off extremely pure, intense light of a single frequency.

Townes said that molecules in space might well be acting like lasers. Laboratory experiments had already shown that when molecules are colliding violently or hit by external radiation they give off or absorb radiation of a precise frequency; the frequency, moreover, varies for every different molecule. But, usually these "fingerprint" emissions fell within the invisible infrared or radio portion of the electromagnetic spectrum. If such emissions were being produced by molecules in space, Townes suggested, it should be relatively simple to find them: all scientists had to do was to tune their radio telescopes to the right frequencies.

That was easier said than done. Tuning a radio telescope with the required accuracy requires considerable care; not only must its circuitry be properly adjusted but the antenna must be of the right shape and material. But even before such tuning of the telescope, the suspected molecule's fingerprint frequency must first be determined in careful laboratory studies. Unlike the casual stargazer, the molecule-hunting radio astronomer cannot rely on serendipity. He must know exactly what he is looking for ahead of time.

The first success in the hunt was chalked up by radio astronomers at the Massachusetts Institute of Technology in 1963. Shortly before, scientists at the University of California in Berkeley had reported finding a new molecule in space, which they dubbed mysterium. But the MIT group showed that the mysterium was not mysterious at all. It was the familiar hydroxyl radical (OH). Consisting of an atom of oxygen and one of hydrogen, it is closely related to water (H_2O), which has an additional hydrogen atom. The discovery created widespread excitement since the presence of such molecular fragments of water hinted that there might also be complete water molecules in space. The presence of water would be profoundly significant for one simple reason: water is an essential ingredient of all life, as we know it.

In 1968, the Berkeley astronomers followed with a triumph of their own. After devising new techniques to suppress background noise in their electronic ears, they detected the fingerprints not only of water but of ammonia (NH_3), a molecule associated with life processes. In the wake of that success, the National Radio Astronomy Observatory's telescopes at Green Bank, West

Virginia, and on Kitt Peak, Arizona, also geared up for the molecule hunt. Bell Laboratories provided some timely help in the form of a new telephone transmission device that could convert the high frequencies of the agitated molecules—which vibrate at billions of hertz (cycles per second)—into more easily detectable signals of about 100 million hertz.

The gadget turned out to be a successful detective. With its help, radio astronomers were soon put on the track of dozens of other molecules, including hydrogen cyanide (HCN), methyl alcohol (CH_3OH), formaldehyde (CH_2O), and dimethyl ether (CH_3OCH_3). In 1971, Leonid N. Weliachew, a visiting French radio astronomer at the California Institute of Technology, found the first signs of extragalactic molecular activity. Turning Caltech's three big dish antennas toward galaxies M82 and NGC253, he picked up the characteristic signals of the hydroxyl radical, perhaps a clue to water-building processes beyond the Milky Way.

These discoveries provided new insights for scientists trying to understand the intricacies of how stars and planets are born in the collapse of clouds of interstellar gases and dust. As the contraction speeds up, the cloud's temperature rises. Yet such heating should tend to halt the collapse and make the cloud expand again. Somehow, if a star is ever to form, the cloud must be able to shed some excess heat during its contraction. Some astronomers think that the radiation given off by the colliding molecules may provide the mechanism that transports heat out of the cloud at this crucial moment in the young star's life. There is good evidence in support of the theory. By far the best hunting grounds for molecules have been in such hot, gaseous regions as the Orion nebula and the Pleiades, both apparently sites of star formation.

Molecule building in space may also tell us something about how life evolved. No one seriously believes that living things exist in the clouds between the stars. Cornell astronomer Carl Sagan's speculations about extraterrestrial life place him in the forefront of the ranks of exobiologists (those who study the possibility of life beyond the earth), yet he acknowledges that there would not be enough collisions of molecules in a cloud in the entire estimated lifetime of the universe to produce even so simple an organism as a virus. Still, it is a fact that chemicals as complex as organic molecules form in space. Moreover, several of the organic molecules discovered are involved in the first chemical steps leading up to the creation of amino acids and proteins, which are the basic building blocks of life. Some radio astronomers, encouraged by the discovery of amino acids in meteorites, think that they may well find the same molecules in space. The only hitch in searching for them is deciding what to listen for. Because amino acids break up easily during spectral studies in the laboratory, it has been difficult to determine their fingerprint frequencies.

Even if no amino acids are ever found in interstellar space, the molecules discovered so far provide convincing proof of an idea that was once little more than science fiction speculation: that the same chemical reactions that produced the first stirrings of life on earth more than 3 billion years ago may be under way throughout our galaxy. This in turn could mean that similar life has formed elsewhere on planets in the Milky Way and even beyond.

9

THE EXPANDING UNIVERSE

More than 2400 years ago the Greek philosopher Democritus thought about the nature of the diffuse cloud of light across the sky that he and his fellow Greeks called the Milky Way. He speculated that it was actually "composed of a multitude of stars so near to each other that their light blended together." It was a shrewd guess, but some 2000 years elapsed before Democritus's suspicions were confirmed. Turning his first crude telescope at the Milky Way, Galileo found that it was indeed made up of separate stars. The discovery did more than to make a prophet out of an ancient philosopher. Coming only a few years after Copernicus had demoted the earth from its central position in the universe and replaced it with the sun, Galileo's observations of the Milky Way opened the door to an even more revolutionary idea: because there were many more stars in the sky than had been suspected, perhaps the sun and its family of planets were not unique.

As telescopes improved, the idea was strengthened.

By the 18th century, astronomers began finding more and more fuzzy little patches of light in the sky that were clearly not stars. Astronomers gave them the catchall name "nebula." Some of the nebulas turned out to be comets, small chunks of matter that make lopsided journeys across the solar system; in one case, a would-be comet turned out to be a new planet, Uranus.

But most nebulas could not be so easily explained. Unlike comets or planets or any other wandering objects in the solar system, they remained stationary against the background of stars, which suggested that they were at least as distant as the stars, perhaps even farther off. In fact, in the middle of the 18th century, the English theologian and scientist Thomas Wright and the German philosopher Immanuel Kant independently concluded that some nebulas were islands of stars far beyond the Milky Way. The idea was so daring for its time that Wright subsequently had doubts and reverted to a more medieval conception of the universe. As he later saw it, the universe consisted of a great spherical cavity in which the earth was at the center and all the nebulas, stars, and comets were distant volcanic eruptions.

Kant appears never to have changed his mind, but he went on to occupy himself with other philosophical questions. In retrospect, his lack of persistence cannot really be faulted. In his day telescopes were still too crude to show any significant detail in the nebulas; nor did astronomers have any sure method of measuring their distance. Without such tools, no one could do more than guess about their nature.

By the beginning of the 20th century, all that had changed. Long and patient observation had persuaded most astronomers that the Milky Way was a great disk of stars, of which the sun was only a minor component. In fact, the idea had been proposed as early as the late 18th century by William Herschel. But a central question remained as the new century opened: Does the

Milky Way comprise the entire universe or are there other star systems in space beyond it?

The answer came gradually through a succession of observations, beginning with those of Henrietta Leavitt of the Harvard College Observatory. A research assistant at the observatory in the early years of the century, she focused her attention on a strange class of stars that periodically brighten and dim, like flickering light bulbs. Now astronomers understand the nature of these pulsations: they are apparently the result of internal instabilities near the star's surface that periodically cause the hot stellar gases to expand and contract in a regular cycle reminiscent of the action in a car's cylinders. The first stars of this category were found in the constellation Cepheus (named after the husband of Cassiopeia and father of Andromeda); hence astronomers called them Cepheid variables or simply Cepheids. Miss Leavitt's Cepheids, however, were located not in that constellation but in the smaller of two star groups in the southern hemisphere's skies called the Magellanic clouds (because they were first reported during Ferdinand Magellan's historic voyage around the globe).

A methodical worker, Miss Leavitt soon noticed a curious pattern in the behavior of the Cepheids: the longer a star glowed between each dimout, the brighter it became. Known as the "period-luminosity" relationship, this seemed to work for all Cepheids. Any two Cepheids that had the same periods—the length of time between successive dimouts—also had the same average luminosity, or brightness.

When Ejnar Hertzsprung heard of her discovery, he quickly realized that it could be put to practical use as a yardstick to gauge the distance of objects in the skies. Until then astronomers depended largely on trigonometric means to measure distances; at best these worked only for relatively nearby stars. To make distance determinations beyond them, astronomers compared the relative brightness of objects. The procedure is complicated, however, by the fact that the true or absolute brightness of celestial bodies, independent of their distance from us, varies greatly. Thus, any time astronomers want to use the apparent brightness of objects in the skies as a measure of distance, they must first determine their absolute brightness.

Miss Leavitt's period-luminosity relationship offered an indirect way of determining absolute brightness. As Hertzsprung pointed out, the behavior of the Cepheids in the Small Magellanic cloud was not likely to be unique; the same pattern should hold for all Cepheids, even those so near that their distances can be determined by more direct means. Once he had that distance, he could calculate their true brightness. Then he could compare Cepheids of known absolute brightness with Cepheids of comparable periods in the Small Magellanic cloud and, by the period-luminosity relationship, figure out their absolute brightness too. With that information in hand, and assuming that all the stars in the cloud were roughly the same distance away, he finally arrived at how far away the Small Magellanic cloud is.

The procedure seemed to work well. After making the required measurements and calculations, Hertzsprung concluded that the Small Magellanic cloud was some 30,000 light-years away, at what would now be recognized as the far edge of the Milky Way.

Other astronomers were slow to appreciate the full significance of Hertzsprung's achievement for two reasons: first, the original figure that he had published came out as only 3000 light-years because of a printer's error; and second, Hertzsprung had slightly miscalculated the brightness of the Cepheids, which also had the effect of underestimating the distance of the Small Magellanic cloud. Now it is known that it is, in fact, some 170,000 light-years away. Even so, Hertzsprung's measurement was an indisputable milestone in astronomy; for it gave the first indication that the Small Magellanic cloud was not part of the Milky Way but a separate galaxy.

A few years later, Harlow Shapley used the same

technique to measure the distance of large, spherical groupings of stars within the Milky Way called globular clusters. His work had important results: by mapping the distribution of the gobular clusters, he was able to show not only that the Milky Way is shaped like a giant lens, but that the sun is sitting near the edge of the lens. Before Shapley's measurements, astronomers were generally agreed that the sun is located near the center of the galaxy. That revision had profound philosophical implications. By shifting the sun's position to a more remote place in the Milky Way, Shapley was also demoting man, making him a little less important in the universal scheme of things, just as Copernicus had done some four centuries earlier.

Still, the overriding question of whether the Milky Way is only one of many galaxies was not settled until the appearance of another gifted astronomer, Edwin P. Hubble. A three-letter athlete in college (boxing, track, and basketball), a former Rhodes scholar and law-school graduate, Hubble had decided belatedly to study astronomy because, as he liked to say, "it was astronomy that mattered." In his doctoral thesis at the University of Chicago, Hubble had already indicated that he thought the smaller nebulas were outside the Milky Way, but the telescope available to him at the university's Yerkes Observatory was not powerful enough to confirm his suspicions. He needed a far bigger eye on the universe.

Such an instrument was about to become available. By the end of 1917, George Ellery Hale had finished directing the difficult task of grinding and installing a 100-inch mirror atop California's Mount Wilson. A mile above the Los Angeles basin, the site could be reached only after a grueling climb up a winding eight-mile mule trail from Pasadena. The telescope was the largest that had yet been built, and Hale sought the best possible people to use it. Having already enticed Harlow Shapley, he also wanted the promising young Hubble on his staff. But Hubble, at the moment, had other things on his mind. The United States had just entered the First World War and, characteristically, Hubble did not want to be left out of the action. "Regret cannot accept your invitation," he telegraphed Hale. "Am off to war."

Hubble served as an army motorcycle driver in France and seems to have enjoyed himself thoroughly. After the signing of the Armistice, he turned back to the more peaceful pursuit of stargazing. Belatedly taking up Hale's offer, he arrived at Mount Wilson in the summer of 1919 and promptly began what would become the chief concern of his scientific career: unraveling the mystery of the nebulas.

By this time, astronomers were already aware that some nebulas, like the great gaseous clouds in Orion, are within the Milky Way; but they were still vigorously debating the true nature and location of the fainter spiral-shaped nebulas. Individual stars had by then been spotted in at least two of the spirals, M31, which is now known as the great galaxy in Andromeda, and its virtual twin M33. Reexamining old photographic plates, astronomers also identified several bright novas, or stellar explosions, in some spirals. But in the absence of any measurements of their distance, no one could say for sure whether the spirals were separate islands of stars or merely knots of stars in the Milky Way.

Hubble tackled the problem slowly and carefully. To prepare himself, he spent two years studying the obviously nearby gaseous nebulas. During that apprenticeship, he also got valuable experience with the big new telescope. From the gaseous nebulas he went on to NGC 6822, an irregularly shaped nebula that had been discovered years earlier by the American astronomer E. E. Barnard. Over the next two years, Hubble photographed NGC 6822 some fifty times. The work was painstaking; usually no more than a single picture could be taken in a night because the nebula's light was so faint that every exposure lasted several hours. Sometimes a single photograph took several nights. All the while, Hubble had to keep NGC 6822 in the telescope's sights. But his patient effort was rewarded. When he finally finished photographing the nebula he counted no fewer than 15 variable stars within it. At least 11 of these were Cepheids. Turning to the familiar relationship between their period and brightness, he calculated NGC 6822's distance: it was some 700,000 light-years away, easily the greatest distance that had been measured by astronomers. Hubble had no doubts about the importance of that measurement. As he wrote in his book *The Realm of the Nebulae,* NGC 6822 was the "first object definitely assigned to a region outside the galactic system."

He now felt ready to turn to the spirals M31 and M33. Again using the Cepheid yardstick, he determined that they were even more distant; each was about 800,000 light-years away. (More recent measurements have shown that Hubble underestimated their distance; astronomers now say that the Andromeda galaxy is some 2 million light-years away.) When Hubble announced his findings to the scientific community in 1925, it ended the great debate. The spiral nebulas were separate galaxies far beyond the Milky Way. In barely six years of observing, Hubble had vastly expanded man's notions about the universe, and in the process he had made man's place in it even more obscure. Not only was the sun an insignificant star, but the Milky Way could hardly be considered unusual any longer.

Hubble's measurements of the distance of M31 and M33 were the first great achievement in his long career. He went on to classify the extragalactic nebulas into major classes—irregular nebulas, like the Magellanic clouds, elliptical nebulas, and spirals—and their subclasses. By then, astronomers had already found that the spectra of the galaxies, like those of stars, displayed light or dark lines at certain frequencies. The lines obviously were the characteristic spectral fingerprints of the chemical elements in the galaxies or the gases surrounding them. But they offer clues not only to a celestial body's composition, but to its movements. If the lines of the spectrum are shifted from their usual place toward the blue end, the object is apparently moving toward the earth. If they are shifted toward the red, it is speeding away from the earth.

The first astronomer to make a systematic investigation of such Doppler shifts in the spectra of galaxies was V. M. Slipher at the Lowell Observatory in Flagstaff, Arizona. In 1912, he examined the spectrum of the Andromeda nebula; it was not called a galaxy until after Hubble determined its great distance. Slipher found that the nebula's light was shifted toward the blue; this meant it was moving toward the earth. He also calculated that it was traveling at nearly 700,000 miles per hour. It was an incredibly high speed, and many people wondered if the nebula would collide with the solar system. Subsequently, astronomers realized that Andromeda's headlong rush toward the earth was an illusion, created by the rotation of the Milky Way's great spiral arms, which seemed to be carrying the sun (along with its family of planets) toward Andromeda. When the Milky Way's rotational velocity was subtracted, Andromeda was found to be receding from us. In fact, except for Andromeda's misleading blue shift, virtually all the nebulas studied by Slipher showed distinct red shifts. His conclusion was that they were all speeding away from the earth.

Recognizing the value of Slipher's work, Hubble continued it with the 100-inch telscope. By 1929, he had not only measured the distances of some two dozen galaxies, but also clocked their speeds. What he found was as startling as his earlier identification of the spirals as separate islands of stars. Based on the red shifts of these galaxies, he determined that they all were speeding away from the Milky Way. Furthermore, this recessional velocity v increased directly with distance $r;$ that is, the farther away the galaxies are, the faster they seem to be moving away. Called Hubble's law, the relationship means that if a galaxy is, say, 400 million light-years away, it will travel twice as fast as a galaxy 200 million light-years away. In mathematical terms, the relationship between velocity and distance can be expressed by the simple equation $v/r = H$, in which H (called the Hubble constant) represents the rate at which the speed increases.

Hubble's work provided unexpected observational support for an idea that was only beginning to be considered by cosmologists—practitioners of a special branch of astronomy that occupies itself with the nature, origin, and future of the universe. In 1916, Einstein published a revolutionary new explanation of gravity that he called the general theory of relativity. It had been devised by Einstein to overcome certain basic difficulties in the old law of gravity that had been set down by Newton nearly three centuries earlier. For example, the Newtonian law could not explain certain peculiarities in the planet Mercury's travels around the sun: on each trip the planet's closest approach to the sun (perihelion) came at a slightly different place in Mercury's elliptical orbit.

Einstein's theory explained that revolving bodies behave slightly differently in their travels through space than can be predicted by Newtonian law. Relativity also forecast two new phenomena. Einstein said that light would not only be bent by a strong gravitational field but be shifted toward the red end of the spectrum. Subsequently verified by actual observations, these effects could be explained by the underlying theme of Einstein's equations. Simply stated, it holds that space is curved by gravity and all considerations of this curvature must take into account a fourth dimension: time.

Out of his mathematical speculations, Einstein constructed a model of the universe that was seemingly limited in size (about 100 million light-years across, he said) and stable and unchangeable over time. But to get such results Einstein had to tamper slightly with his own equations. They had suggested an unstable, changing universe. Einstein, who was convinced that the universe was unchanging, could not accept such a picture. To make his model fit his deep-seated convictions, he introduced a new force into his theory. It was a kind

1. The great galaxy (M31) in Andromeda, the Milky Way's cosmic neighbor

2. Cluster of galaxies in the constellation Serpens (*above*)

3. The 200-inch telescope at Palomar Observatory, the largest eye on the heavens (*opposite page*)

4. The Orion nebula, birth-place of new stars (*above*)

5. Peter van de Kamp of Swarthmore College's Sproul Observatory showing a model of a visible star circled by an unseen companion (*opposite page*)

6. Karl Jansky and his pioneering "carousel," a rotating antenna (*right*)

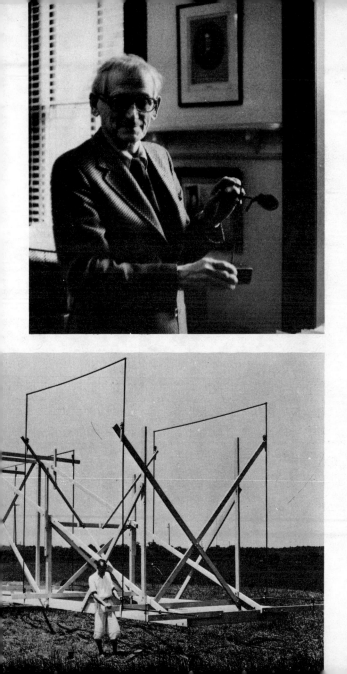

7. Jansky pointing to the position of incoming signals

8. Grote Reber beside the reconstruction of his original "pie plate" telescope at Green Bank, West Virginia (*above*)

9. The 330-foot radio telescope near Bonn, West Germany (*below*)

10. The huge telescope installation carved out of a natural valley at Arecibo, Puerto Rico

11. Edward Purcell (*right*) and Harold Ewen at the dedication of the Harvard Observatory's 60-foot dish antenna radio telescope; Purcell is leaning on the cone-shaped receiver with which they picked up the "song of hydrogen"

12. Pioneer 11 approaching the rings of Saturn (*opposite page, top*)

13. A storm erupting on the sun's "surface": the extremely bright areas represent the heart of the disturbance; the dark features are a string of sunspots. This photograph was taken July 2, 1974 (*opposite page, bottom*)

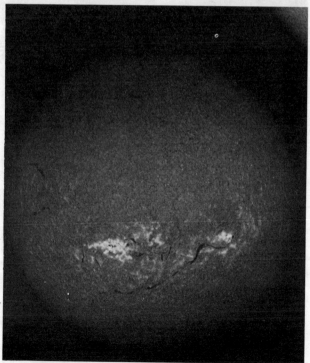

14. A multiple radio source (NGC5128) in the constellation Centaurus; it is possibly two galaxies in upheaval (*opposite page, top*)

15. Another case of galactic turmoil (M87), in Virgo (*opposite page, bottom*)

16. An especially bright Seyfert galaxy (NGC4151)

17. The 100-inch telescope at Mount Wilson Observatory, used by Hubble to measure galactic distances

21. A typical spiral galaxy (M74, in Pisces), similar to the Milky Way

22. Jesse Greenstein at the 200-inch Palomar telescope

23. Margaret Burbridge, one of the first quasar hunters (*this page, top*)

24. Maarten Schmidt explaining how he discovered the red shift of a quasar (*this page, bottom*)

25. A quasar (3C 273) with a jet of material streaming from it (*opposite page*)

26. The quasar-hunting Goldstone antenna in the Mojave Desert of southern California

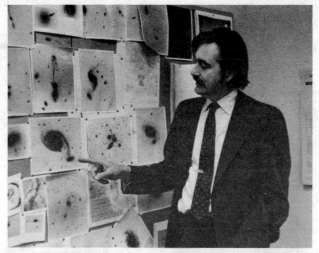

27. Halton Arp pointing to a photograph of a galaxy seemingly linked to a quasar (*top photo*)

28. The Crab nebula in Taurus, remnants of an exploded star

29. Astronomer John Brandt inspecting ancient Indian pictographs near Zuni, New Mexico; he believes that the cross above the crescent moon (*left*) represented the supernova of 1054 A.D.

30. Fritz Zwicky, who postulated neutron stars years before they were discovered

31. Subrahmanyan Chandrasekhar, pioneer astrophysicist who thought the "impossible" was possible

32. Jocelyn Bell at Cambridge, England, after the first pulsar was found

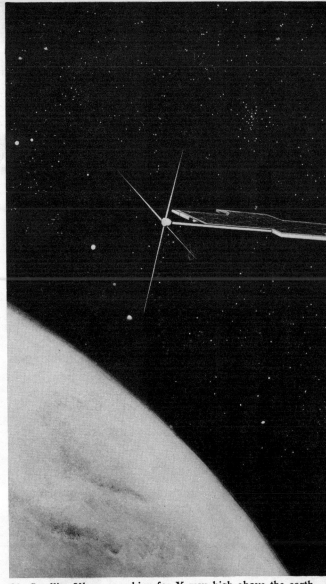

33. Satellite *Uhuru* searching for X rays high above the earth

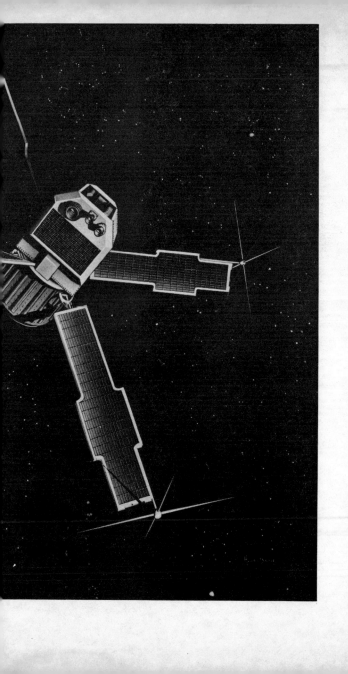

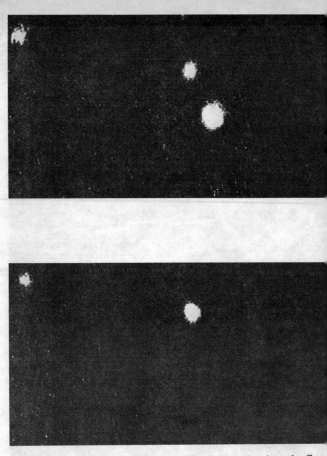

34. The pulsar in the Crab nebula, flashing on (*top*) and off (*bottom*)

35. A black hole (*right*) drawing off material from a super-giant star

36. Allan Sandage lecturing on the age of the universe (*above*)

37. John A. Wheeler discussing contemporary astronomical themes (*below*)

of cosmic repulsion that kept his universe fixed in total size, yet let changes take place within it. In his equations, this universal braking force was represented by a new factor called the cosmological constant.

Before long Einstein had every reason to regret this mathematical sleight of hand. Studying Einstein's equations, the Dutch mathematician Willem de Sitter realized that they indicated a universe steadily growing in size. The Russian mathematician Alexander Friedmann had even worse news for Einstein. He found a fundamental error. As algebra students everywhere know, it is permissible to divide both sides of an equation by the same number except when that number is 0. What Einstein had overlooked, Friedmann explained, was that the cosmological constant sometimes became 0, yet Einstein had divided by it. Incredible as it now seems, the brilliant Einstein had erred in solving his own equations. If the cosmological constant were eliminated, Friedmann said, a different universe would emerge that could either contract or expand.

While theoreticians were arguing over the solution to Einstein's equations, Hubble dropped a bombshell. Everywhere he looked out into space, he said, the galaxies seemed to be flying away from us. Even more amazing, the most distant galaxies were the fastest-moving. Out of these observations only one conclusion seemed possible: the universe is expanding. Far back in time, a cataclysmic event, perhaps an explosion, scattered the components of the universe in different directions. Those components, the galaxies, are still flying apart, like spots on an expanding balloon. Curiously, an observer traveling on any of these spots would think all the other spots were moving away from him. But so would his neighbors on any other spot. For example, while the Andromeda galaxy seems to be moving away from us, astronomers on that distant galaxy would observe the Milky Way as moving away from them.

In one fell sweep, Hubble's findings resolved the debate about Einstein's equations. The universe was indeed expanding, and Einstein himself later confessed to the Russian-American physicist George Gamow, who had been Friedmann's student, that the cosmological constant had been the biggest blunder of his career.

Hubble discussed his dramatic observations in a paper published by the National Academy of Sciences in Washington in 1929, but even before then the Belgian priest-astronomer Abbé Georges Lemaître had already evolved a theory for how he thought the universe began. All matter, he said, was originally highly compressed into an extremely hot "primeval atom"—or cosmic egg, as it was subsequently called by Gamow. The clump was only about thirty times as large across as the sun. But as it expanded outward in an explosion of unimaginable magnitude the material thinned and cooled; in some places it contracted into galaxies and stars. The galaxies are still flying apart (although their gravity lets them retain their individual shapes).

Elaborating on Lemaître's scenario, Gamow called the original explosion the Big Bang. When it began, Lemaître's primeval atom consisted of protons, neutrons, and electrons. But within half an hour, Gamow's calculations showed, the explosion had produced most of the hydrogen and helium in the universe as well as some of the heavier elements. To buttress his argument for skeptics Gamow pointed out that mankind has already witnesed such events on a much smaller scale. Only a fraction of a second after its detonation, an atomic bomb produces a wide variety of fission products.

How long ago did the Big Bang occur? Hubble's work provides a plausible clock. According to his law, the velocity at which the galaxies are moving away from each other is increasing at a constant rate H. If a scientist wants to date the Big Bang, he must calculate how long the galaxies have been flying apart. The calculation is simple: he divides the distance that any particular galaxy has traveled r by its velocity v. The quotient is the galaxy's travel time T, or the age of the universe. (As it happens, r/v is the reciprocal of the calculation v/r used to obtain the Hubble constant H. Thus, if one knows H one can readily obtain T, since $1/H = T$.)

Hubble himself reckoned the age of the universe as 2 billion years. But scientists immediately questioned the figure. By the 1930s, geological evidence indicated that the earth and hence the sun and the rest of the universe were considerably older. The apparent contradiction between the astronomical and geological dating was resolved in 1952 by Hubble's successor, Walter Baade. Using the 200-inch telescope at Palomar, which Hubble helped design, Baade proved that there are two distinctly different populations, or types, of stars (including the Cepheids), which are unlike in age and brightness. (The first hint of these differences came during World War II; when the Los Angeles area was blacked out as a precaution against air raids, Baade found that the performance of the old 100-inch Mount Wilson telescope was so improved that it could detect hitherto unresolvable galactic details.) The distances derived from Type II Cepheids are correct for the Milky Way, Baade pointed out, but not for Andromeda, which he was working on, or presumably other galaxies. The stars that Hubble and others had used as yardsticks to these galaxies are really Type I Cepheids. Their absolute brightness was much greater than Hubble had thought; hence he greatly underestimated their distance (and overestimated the value of the Hubble constant). The recalibration inspired by Baade's observations made the universe at least 5 billion years old. And since his work, the age of the universe has been revised upward again. In fact, the value of the Hubble constant has been changed so often that astronomers sometimes playfully call it the Hubble variable. But periodic revisions do not reflect any flaws in Hubble's theory of the expanding universe, only difficulties in measuring the extremely faint light of distant galaxies. Late in 1974, after years of observation atop Palomar mountain using the latest photographic techniques, astronomer Allan Sandage announced a new value for the Hubble constant. According to Sandage, upon whom has fallen Hubble's mantle at the Hale Observatories, the universe was even older than hitherto suspected.

10

THE MYSTERY
OF THE QUASARS

By the end of the 1950s, radio astronomers had already made so many remarkable discoveries that new and bigger radio telescopes were being built everywhere. Although these electronic ears were more sensitive and could pick up more detail, one goal still eluded radio astronomers. No radio source in the skies had been indentified with a visual object that was smaller than a galaxy or a cloud of swirling gases, except for the nearby sun and Jupiter. As carefully as they listened, radio astronomers could not detect a radio star.

In 1960, the situation dramatically changed. Using precise new coordinates from Jodrell Bank's big dish for a strong radio source known as 3C 48 (after its designation as the 48th object in the third Cambridge radio survey), Palomar's Allan Sandage aimed the 200-inch telescope at the location in the sky. With the help of a colleague, Thomas Matthews, he quickly picked out 3C 48's optical counterpart on the photographic plate. It is a relatively faint, bluish "star" that cannot be seen by the unaided eye. Shortly thereafter, optical astronomers, guided by more precise fixes from radio astronomers, found several other starlike objects that give off radio signals.

The objects had everyone baffled. They were such powerful radio emitters that they did not seem to be nearby stars, since no stars close to the solar system or anywhere else in the galaxy had been identified with strong radio sources. But they also seemed much too small to be distant galaxies. To complicate matters, when Caltech's Jesse Greenstein analyzed their light, he found that it was unusually rich in ultraviolet wavelengths, yet the spectral lines were unlike any the experienced observer had seen before.

While scientists pondered the strange nature of these starlike radio sources, radio astronomer Cyril Hazard set about performing an ingenious experiment with the big 210-foot Parkes dish antenna in Australia. He wanted to locate radio source 3C 273 precisely enough so optical astronomers could use the fix to find the object. Along with the big telescope Hazard made use of the earth's nearest neighbor, the moon. Over the centuries the moon's movements have been so carefully studied that astronomers know exactly where it is at any time in its monthly passage around the earth.

During its travels the moon passes in front of many stars, briefly blotting out their radiation. As it happens, one of the objects that appears occasionally on the moon's path is 3C 273. All Hazard had to do to find its precise location in the sky was to time when 3C 273's signals were blocked by the moon's leading edge and when they reappeared from behind the moon's trailing limb.

The experiment was successful, and when Hazard passed on 3C 273's new coordinates to the Dutch-born optical astronomer Maarten Schmidt, a colleague of Greenstein's at Caltech, Schmidt had no trouble finding the object on existing photographic plates. No one had taken it for more than an undistinguished blue star. Although it was not especially bright, it could even be seen with small amateur telescopes with diameters of only 6 inches.

But when Schmidt turned the 200-inch mirror on 3C 273, it emerged as a far more complex object. The radio probing by the Australians had already indicated that it consisted of two distinct sources. On Schmidt's photographic plates it also had two components; the bulk of 3C 273 consisted of a fuzzy, round starlike object, but a dim jet trailed out of one side. (Radio studies later showed that while the jet is much fainter than the central region in visible light, it accounts for 90 percent of 3C 273's radio energy.) Schmidt also found that the object was brighter than any of four similar radio sources studied by his colleagues at Palomar.

In spite of their vague resemblance to stars, however, it seemed abundantly clear that these radio-emitting objects were not stars in any conventional sense. For lack of a better name radio astronomers called them quasi-stellar (meaning starlike) radio sources, while optical astronomers dubbed them quasi-stellar objects. But soon these cumbersome titles were shortened by the Chinese-American astrophysicist Hong-Yee Chiu into a word that is now firmly part of the astronomers' vocabulary: quasars.

The mystery of the quasars quickly deepened as Schmidt began to study 3C 273. The tall, extremely careful observer managed to obtain a reasonably good spectrum of 3C 273's faint light, and like Greenstein, he was totally bewildered by what he saw: the spectral lines did not resemble those of any other heavenly object. Greenstein was already beginning to evolve his own explanation for quasars: he thought that they might be extremely dense objects in our galaxy, possibly the remnants of a great stellar explosion. But Schmidt continued to ponder the strange spectrum. After six weeks, he had one of those flashes of insight that make scientific history. Is it possible, he asked himself, that the spectral lines are so unfamiliar because they have been shifted to the red end of the spectrum?

His suspicions had been aroused by three curious lines in 3C 273's spectrum. Although they resembled the familiar fingerprints of hydrogen, they were located, not at the blue end of the spectrum, where such lines are usually found, but at the other end among the red wavelengths. To confirm his hunch, Schmidt proposed a test. The strongest of hydrogen's characteristic spectral lines, the H-alpha line, seemed to be missing from the quasar's visible light. But, as Schmidt pointed out, if the light had undergone a red shift, the missing line should show up even farther off in the invisible infrared region of the spectrum. To Schmidt's delight, his colleague Beverley Oke had already examined the quasar's spectrum with an electronic device that could detect its infrared wavelengths. Exactly where Schmidt told him to look, Oke found a band that bore an unmistakable resemblance to the missing H-alpha line.

Schmidt later recalled in interviews with *Time* magazine that the discovery of 3C 273's red shift left him "in a complete state of shock." Other astronomers could readily understand why. Schmidt's measurements showed that the wavelengths of the quasar's light had been stretched no less than 16 percent, which meant that the object was traveling some 29,000 miles per second, presumably as part of the general expansion of the universe. Furthermore, by applying Hubble's law ($r = v/H$) Schmidt could readily calculate 3C 273's distance from earth. It turned out to be some 1.5 billion light-years away, almost as far as some of the most distant galaxies.

Quickly shelving his own theory that quasars might be nearby objects, Greenstein reexamined the spectrum of 3C 48, the first of the quasars, and suddenly its baffling lines became embarrassingly clear. They also had been red-shifted—by an amount three times as great as 3C 273's lines. According to Hubble's law, the quasar was 3.6 billion light-years away.

As astronomers everywhere vied to find quasars with even larger red shifts, the search took on a competitive look. By December 1966, using the Lick Observatory's 120-inch telescope, British-born astronomer Margaret Burbridge found a quasar with a red shift that indicated it was racing away from the Milky Way at 81.2 percent of the speed of light. Only a month later, Schmidt regained leadership in the quasar race by finding a red shift that was slightly larger. "I feel a little embarrassed about it," Schmidt said at the time. "This thing has to be just 1 percent above Margaret's." Greenstein eased his embarrassment by honoring him with a case of wine.

By 1973, Burbridge and her colleague at Lick, E. Joseph Wampler, regained the record by measuring a red shift of 353 percent in a quasar designated OQ (for the University of Ohio's quasar catalogue) 172. According to the Hubble rules, it was racing away at more than 90 percent of the speed of light. Equally remarkable, the red shift suggested that the quasar might be at the limits of the observable universe.

To be visible over such staggering distances, astronomers calculated, the quasar would have to be shining as brightly as one hundred galaxies, each filled with billions of stars. Yet, incredibly, every indication is that quasars are remarkably compact; in fact, they hardly seem much bigger than stars. One clue to their size is a curious flickering in their light. Some quasars dim and brighten again in periods as short as a month. By simple physical rules, such an object cannot have a diameter of more than a light-month—the distance light travels in a month. By contrast, normal galaxies are thousands of light-years across. To understand why quasars can only be a small fraction of that size, one can think of them as enormous celestial chandeliers. Even if all the bulbs in such a cosmic "chandelier" were turned off simultaneously, we would see light from it as long as a month after the bulbs stopped burning; it would take that long for the light on the farthest side of the chandelier to reach us. Thus a celestial object that brightens and dims cannot be any larger than the distance light is able to travel during one fluctuation.

Schmidt calculated that the tiny quasars had to be burning up as much energy in a single year as the sun does in its entire lifetime to be visible at their great distances. But where did the compact objects get their fuel? Trying to provide an answer, scientists proposed any number of explanations. Fred Hoyle and his Caltech colleague William Fowler imaginatively suggested that quasars might be superstars that had reached the end of their life. Collapsing under its own enormous weight, the infalling material of the superstar would generate so much heat and other radiation that it would shine as brightly as a quasar. But skeptics quickly objected. Schmidt and Greenstein showed that the gravitational pull of such a massive star would be strong enough to distort the shape of the Milky Way. Others said that it might crush itself out of existence, leaving nothing behind except a ghostly remnant called a black hole.

Another intriguing idea was that quasars might be a series of stellar explosions in a tightly packed clump of stars. As one star erupted, it would trigger the explosion of its immediate neighbor, as in a chain reaction of a nuclear reactor. Another explanation was that quasars might be created by the annihilation of matter and antimatter. Such an encounter could be far more violent than conventional nuclear reactions because all the matter and antimatter involved would be converted into energy. A few daring theorists even speculated that quasars might be entry ports—"white holes" —for alien antimatter from another universe. Initial observational support for the idea came from University of Arizona astronomer Frank Low. An expert in infrared observations, which are best made high above the atmosphere (where there is no obscuring moisture), he has studied galaxies and quasars from jet planes and found that their centers seem to be giving off enormous amounts of infrared radiation—far more than could be readily accounted for by ordinary physical processes. These observations have since been questioned, but the energy output from galactic centers remains a puzzle. Perhaps the most exciting explanation for quasars is that they are leftovers from the Big Bang. The possibility is not so unlikely as it might seem. If quasars are really as distant as is believed, their light has been traveling billions of years to reach the earth. Thus in studying that light, astronomers are not only looking across great distances, but probing far back in time. What they see began its journey long before the earth or the sun came into being. Possibly the source of the light does not even exist any more. At the very least, the quasar has undergone enormous changes during those billions of years.

In most of their speculations about quasars, astronomers have been guided by an underlying assumption: that the red shifts of quasars are cosmological, or caused by the general expansion of the universe. But the red shifts could also be produced by other means that do not necessarily involve the expansion of the universe or even very high speeds. If so, quasars might be relatively nearby, perhaps even within the Milky Way. More important, it would mean that quasars are not as bright as they seem, and astronomers would not have to rack their brains figuring out how they give off such prodigious outbursts of energy.

One of the first astronomers to question the cosmological nature of red shifts was Fred Hoyle. He had every reason for wanting to bring the quasars closer to earth. At stake was his Steady State theory of the universe. Contrary to the Big Bang theory, it holds that the universe has no beginning and no end; it has always existed and will continue to exist forever. Hoyle and his colleagues, Hermann Bondi and Thomas Gold, do not deny that the galaxies are moving apart, but they contend that new matter is constantly being created to fill the spaces in the void; the overall density of matter remains the same. How such creation occurs or what happens to old galaxies Hoyle cannot say. But, as defenders of the Steady State theory like to point out, their opponents cannot tell what caused the Big Bang or what preceded Lemaître's cosmic egg either. So, in a deeper philosophical sense, the Steady

State has as much claim to validity—perhaps even more—than the Big Bang, which depends on a possibly unique, one-time event.

In any case, since the number of quasars seems to increase at greater distances, they challenge the Steady State theory. For if the universe has no beginning or end, as the Steady State contends, it should always look the same, both now and in the past. Yet if the quasar population varies over distance—and time— these strange objects suggest that the universe once looked considerably different and perhaps was more densely packed together. Such evidence clearly favors the Big Bang.

To rescue his theory, Hoyle looked for other explanations of the red shifts. Citing Einstein's general theory of relativity, he pointed out that light could be shifted to the red end of the spectrum under the influence of a powerful gravitational field. Perhaps the collapsing superstar envisioned by him and Fowler could turn such a relativistic trick. As the star's light struggled to free itself from the star's strong gravity, it would, in effect, have to work harder to escape than light leaving a smaller star, just as a rocket has to work harder to leave the earth's gravitational field than the moon's. During its exertion, the light loses energy; its frequency drops and its wavelengths stretch to the weaker or red end of the spectrum.

Such a gravitational red shift occurs in the sun's light, although it is so slight that it is barely detectable. To produce red shifts as large as those in quasars requires a star with 100 million times as much mass as the sun's, and even the inventive Hoyle has been hard-pressed to explain how such gargantuan objects could exist. To make matters worse for the Steady State, it seems to be in direct conflict with another discovery of major importance at Bell Labs, Jansky's old employer. In 1965, while experimenting with a new communications satellite system, Bell scientists Arno Penzias and Robert Wilson picked up a faint, nagging background noise in their sensitive horn-shaped antenna; it seemed to be coming from all parts of the sky with equal intensity. Analysis by physicists showed that these microwaves packed energy equivalent to heat at a temperature of barely 3 degrees above absolute zero. Only a short time before, theorists had predicted that the lingering heat from the Big Bang should now have precisely that temperature. Thus, like the faint red glow in a cooling furnace, the newly discovered background radiation provides one more piece of persuasive evidence in favor of the Big Bang. The radiation apparently is the leftover heat from the great fires of that cataclysmic explosion.

Noncosmological red shifts can be produced by effects other than gravitational ones. For instance, speed alone causes spectral shifts. Thus, if quasars were fragments of material expelled at high velocities from nearby galaxies or even from objects within the Milky Way, their light would show red shifts. Photographs of several galaxics—M82, for example—indicate that they are being ripped apart by violent internal upheavals. Some astronomers have even suggested that such galaxies in turmoil can eject fragments into space at velocities close to the speed of light. Hence, the light from the ejected material would also be greatly red-shifted.

No one has argued the case for such an explanation of quasars more persistently than Halton Arp, another Hale Observatories astronomer who regularly works with the 200-inch Palomar telescope. In a number of photographs he has found that quasars seem to be linked by wispy threads of material with neighboring galaxies. What makes the photographs even more interesting is that the quasars have much higher red shifts than their "companion" galaxies. Arp has a ready explanation for the difference; he says that the quasars may have been tossed off by the galaxies at very high velocities. Not only would his theory explain the higher red shifts; it would also account for the apparent wispy connection between the galaxies and quasars, since such a high-speed eviction would presumably leave behind a trail of debris.

Other astronomers, including many of his colleagues at Palomar, strongly dispute Arp's interpretation. Questioning the reality of the apparent bridge between the quasars and galaxies, they say that such effects may simply be quirks of the photographic plate or optical illusions. They contend that Arp may be looking at objects that lie along the telescope's line of sight, but at greatly varying distances. Thus the galaxies could be near and the quasars far off even though they appear to be next to each other. In addition, if quasars are being ejected, shrapnel-like, from galaxies, some of them presumably would be flying in the direction of the earth, and displaying blue shifts in their light. Yet of the quasars discovered so far, all show red shifts.

After years of close study, quasars remain as mysterious as ever. Perhaps the majority of astronomers are willing to accept the red shifts as cosmological, if only because other explanations conflict with the well-accepted idea of an expanding universe. But they admit that they are hard put to account for the enormous energy output of distant quasars without stretching accepted physical laws.

In recent years some theorists seeking a conventional energy source for distant quasars have suggested other ideas. MIT physicist Philip Morrison, for one, says that quasars may be nuclei of very ancient, turbulent galaxies, possibly with rotating black holes at their cores. Schmidt, who believes that the red shifts are a true measure of the great distance of quasars, also "guesses" that what we are now seeing as quasars may be galaxies during their violent birth processes. There are some strong clues to support Schmidt's guess: recently astronomers have been finding similarities between the energy processes of quasars, radio galaxies, and the compact Seyfert galaxies. All give indications of violent activity in their bright centers. In addition, quasars have apparently been found in the center of a more ordinary spherical galaxy in the constellation Lacerta, the lizard. To many astronomers these signs indicate that quasars can be a definite stage in the life and evolution of a galaxy.

But other scientists think that quasars—and their red shifts—may have a totally unexpected origin beyond the ken of present knowledge. As the British-born astrophysicist Geoffrey Burbridge bluntly stated in an interview: "We're egomaniacs to say that we know all there is to know about physics." In fact, a hint of a new physics at work in quasars was discovered by radio astronomers in the spring of 1971 during a long-baseline interferometry experiment involving MIT's Haystack antenna in Massachusetts and the National Aeronautics and Space Administration's big dish in California's Mojave Desert. Looking at a number of quasars, the radio astronomers found that their components apparently are flying apart at speeds greatly exceeding the velocity of light, which has long been regarded as the universe's absolute speed limit. At other times they seem to vanish entirely and new ones appear. The radio astronomers cannot say for sure whether the measurements represent true speed or an illusion created by other weird effects, possibly related to the time warps predicted by relativity theory. But the observations add one more mystery to the succession of mysteries about quasars.

All of which has prompted Jesse Greenstein to take up his poet's pen and compose a witty lament that has been displayed on the Caltech blackboards.

Horrid quasar,
Near or far,
This truth to you I must confess:
    My heart for you is full of hate.
O superstar,
Imploded gas,
You glowing speck upon a plate,
    Of Einstein's world you've made a mess!

11

THE DEATH OF STARS

In the summer of A.D. 1054 a new star flared up in the constellation Taurus. Europeans were so occupied fighting each other at the time that they seem to have taken no special notice of the heavenly spectacle, even though the star was so bright it could be seen in daylight. Nor did the Muslims, who, in spite of their great tradition of stargazing, were then busy extending their conquests in Africa. But sharp-eyed court astronomers in China did make a record of the event, as did other sky watchers in Japan, Korea, and even in Arizona, California, and New Mexico, where recently discovered rock carvings show that the Indians there were also awed by the new star.

"Prostrating myself," announced Yang Wei-te, the chief computer of the calendar, to the Sung emperor in Peking, "I have observed the appearance of a guest star." For 23 days that summer the reddish-white star glowed so brilliantly it was "visible by day, like Venus" over the Chinese capital. After a month it began to fade, but it could still be seen at night for nearly two years.

112

Today we know the "guest star" as one of the most intriguing objects in the sky. To the unaided eye the Crab nebula appears as no more than the faintest blur near the tip of the bull's right horn in Taurus. But in the big mirrors on the mountaintops of California, the true picture of the Crab emerges: it is a great cloud of turbulent gases rushing off in all directions at speeds of 700 miles per second. The heavenly guest is not a newborn star, but the remnants of an old star that has experienced a violent death.

The first astronomer to show the link between the Crab nebula and the Chinese guest star was Edwin Hubble. In the late 1920s, he reckoned the rate at which the gases were expanding and concluded that the explosion occurred about 900 years earlier, at the time and place recorded by the Chinese. But the first really serious investigations of such stellar explosions were begun a few years later by Hubble's colleagues at Mount Wilson, Fritz Zwicky and Walter Baade, who began their search not in the Milky Way but in the galaxies beyond it. They had no trouble tracking down what they were looking for. For a brief time, the exploding stars that they found burned so brightly that they gave off as much light as all the billions of other stars in the galaxy combined. Zwicky and Baade named these outbursts supernovas; that was to distinguish them from smaller explosions called novas (Latin for "new") because astronomers originally thought they were newborn stars.

In any one galaxy, supernovas seemed to be relatively rare events, occurring only once or twice a century. Looking back in history, astronomers now realize that the novas observed by the Danish astronomer Tycho Brahe in 1572, which he described in his book *De Nova Stella* (On the New Star), and by Johannes Kepler in 1604 were really supernovas, as was the Chinese guest star in 1054. Still another may have taken place in about 1700, at the site of a powerful radio source in Cassiopeia, but its light was unobserved, apparently because it was dimmed by

interstellar dust. Since then other unwitnessed supernovas may have occurred in remote parts of the
Milky Way that are not readily visible from earth.

Besides collaborating with Baade on supernovas,
Zwicky made a perceptive comment about them. He
said that such explosions would so thoroughly crush
the star's core that the atoms within it would lose their
old identity. Ordinarily the atom's nucleus and its
orbiting electrons are kept apart by the strong nuclear
repulsive force between them. But Zwicky said that
the implosion at the center of the star during a supernova would be powerful enough to drive the electrons
into the nucleus so that they would combine with its
protons. The result would be neutral particles called
neutrons. In fact, said Zwicky, where once there was
a star there would be nothing left but a tiny, densely
packed clump of neutrons.

Zwicky's forecast attracted scant attention in the
1930s. Only a few farsighted theoreticians were beginning to look into what may happen when a star
runs out of its life-giving nuclear fuel. Among the
pioneers in the study of stellar death were the Russian
physicist Lev Landau, the Indian-born physicist Subrahmanyan Chandrasekhar, and the American physicist J. Robert Oppenheimer, who subsequently went
on to direct the manufacture of the first atomic bomb
in World War II. Because of their work, as well as
more recent studies, astronomers can now describe in
dramatic detail the death throes of stars.

Basically, the life of a star ends as it begins. Both
events are controlled by the universe's most pervasive
force: gravity. Tugged by their mutual gravitational
attraction, the clouds of dust and gases that give birth
to stars collapse until their thermonuclear fires ignite.
In the sun reactions began at temperatures of 10 million to 20 million degrees K. At this point, the sun
radiated enough heat outward to counteract the in-
ward pull of gravity, fixing its diameter at about 1 million miles.

But the delicate balance between gravity and heat is

maintained only as long as the star's thermonuclear fires continue. Eventually, the star's principal fuel, hydrogen, runs low. Though the sun is consuming hydrogen at the huge rate of 500 million tons a second, the star will not exhaust its supply for another 5 billion years. But even before all the hydrogen is gone, gravity will dominate again. As the thermonuclear fires dwindle, it will begin to compress the star, driving up temperatures at the core to as high as 100 million degrees K. The helium "ash" created in years of thermonuclear reactions will suddenly ignite and start fusing together to form still heavier atoms.

Before this "helium flash" there will also be changes in the sun's external appearance. Driven by its internal heat, the star will start expanding; its color will slowly change from yellow to orange to red. When the star's diameter has swollen about fifty times, it will be recognizable as a red giant. Following the helium flash, the star may partly collapse again and dim. But the setback should be very brief, perhaps no more than a few hours. As the thermonuclear fires in its interior settle down to "burning" heavier elements, the sun should resume its growth. In the next 30 million years, it will expand to perhaps 400 times its present diameter. All the inner planets out to Mars wil be swallowed up by the expanding giant.

But eventually the giant must stop growing. The sun's expansion will stop when its core becomes loaded with carbon. Although carbon and even heavier elements can be fused by more massive stars, the sun's temperature will not reach the level necessary for a carbon flash. Instead, the sun's fires will diminish, and the heat that sustains the star against the force of its gravity will become increasingly scarce. No longer opposed by the sun's fires, gravity will win the final battle.

For a star of solar mass, the outcome will be simple. In a mere 50,000 years, the star will fall in on itself in a collapse that may be marked by some minor explosions—of the nova type; certainly, nothing as spectacular as a supernova awaits the sun. The sun's interior temperatures and density will climb sharply to act as a brake against further gravitational collapse. But by then the sun will be a shadow of its former self, a small, extremely dense sphere about the size of the earth. A teaspoonful of its material will weigh about 15,000 tons; the atoms inside will be so tightly packed that they will be barely recognizable, forming what physicists call degenerate matter. The sun will be a white dwarf, like the tiny companion of the Dog Star Sirius, which was discovered in 1862 and is sometimes called the Pup.

Initially, the sun will be very bright, radiating significant amounts of heat. But as the white dwarf drifts through space, it will have no major new energy supplies to draw on. Heating by further gravitational collapse will be impossible because the dwarf's atoms will be so tightly packed that no more contraction can take place. The behavior of the star's dense matter will be guided by the "exclusion principle," set forth by the Austrian physicist Wolfgang Pauli, which says, roughly, that no two electrons can occupy the same orbital slot in the atom at the same time. Nor will the star get more heat from its exhausted thermonuclear fires.

Steadily cooling, the dwarf will change color, like an ember, from its original white to orange, then to red, and finally to black. At the end of its life, the sun will be no more than a dark, cold cinder called a black dwarf, destined to wander endlessly round the galaxy.

Yet much stranger fate awaits stars that begin their lives with significantly more mass than the sun. Burning brighter and more quickly, such stars may use up the bulk of their fuel in only a few million years, compared with the sun's life span of many billions of years. Their end will be much more violent than the sun's.

Consider the case of a star at least 40 percent heavier than the sun, but no more than about twice its mass; the exact range is still debated by scientists. When this star has burned off most of its original hydrogen fuel, it too begins to collapse under its own weight, but because of its greater mass there is more compression and more heat. Thermonuclear ignition will not stop with the helium flash; the core of the star becomes so hot that elements beyond helium are fused, forming increasingly heavier nuclei. The reactions create so much heat that the thermonuclear fires spread to the star's outer layers, which are normally too cool in stars like the sun to allow fusion. Finally, the star's temperatures will climb so high that it becomes extremely unstable, like a stick of dynamite. The slightest disturbance can trigger an explosion.

The critical moment comes when the star's reactions start producing iron. Because of their particular structure, iron atoms cannot be combined into heavier elements without consuming energy. As a result, fusion comes to a halt. The core begins to break down into simpler, lighter atoms, and the star's temperature drops.

Astrophysicist Hong-Yee Chiu compares what happens next to the burning of a building with a fireproof roof. When the walls have finally burned away, the roof collapses onto the fire, creating a huge splash of flames. Inside the star, there is similar chaos. No longer supported by internal heat, the star's outer layer will collapse. The fall creates such great pressures on the star's core that its electrons are driven right into its atomic nuclei, as if there were no such barrier as the exclusion principle. For a brief instant temperatures will climb to hundreds of billions of degrees. The heat creates a flood of nearly massless particles called neutrinos, which can ordinarily pass through almost any barrier. But the collapsing layers of the star are so dense that they stop the particles and turn their energy back into heat. Temperatures rise still higher in the star, blasting its outer layers off into space. These calamitous events may take only a few quick seconds, but the energy released is equal to that from billions upon billions of hydrogen bombs. To distant observers, the exploding star may briefly glow as brightly as the entire galaxy. Even astronomers on far-off galaxies should be able to recognize the stellar eruption as a supernova.

In about a month, the supernova's original brilliance will have dimmed, but the hot, glowing gases rushing from the site of the cataclysm will remain visible for hundreds and even thousands of years. Eventually they too will vanish as they spread out through space and become part of the interstellar debris out of which future stars will be born. For even in death the doomed star is part of the eternal process of rebirth and renewal.

Where the great star itself once was, the only thing left will be what Zwicky had predicted: a tiny ball of neutrons. Although the star was originally larger than the sun, its cadaver will be only about 10 miles in diameter. The material will be so incredibly condensed that even a fragment no bigger than a sugar cube will weigh a billion tons, more than an entire fleet of battleships. The huge luminous sphere of gases will have become a neutron star.

Do such unbelievably dense objects really exist in the heavens? By the 1960s, astronomers had a reasonably good understanding of the mechanisms of stellar collapse. They had also observed many supernovas in other galaxies, although none had been seen in the Milky Way since Kepler's supernova in 1604. But the existence of neutron stars was openly questioned. Some scientists regarded them as little more than a mathematical fiction, a convenient solution to the complex equations that describe the collapse of a large star. Others pointed out that even if neutron stars are formed in supernovas, they would be much too small to be detected.

It was in the midst of this debate, during the late 1960s, that British radio astronomers made a discovery that took scientists everywhere by complete surprise. The event was another classic instance of scientific serendipity, a finding that came during unrelated activities.

A few years earlier, Anthony Hewish and his group

at Cambridge University's Mullard Radio Astronomy Observatory had realized that radio stars "twinkle," somewhat like ordinary stars, when their light is disturbed by the earth's restless atmosphere. The twinkling, or scintillation, of the radio sources is a fluctuation in signal strength caused by the passage of the radio waves through the clouds of charged particles from the sun known as the solar wind. But the twinkling occurs so rapidly that it cannot be detected by ordinary radio astronomy techniques. To measure the effect Hewish and his colleagues set up a new telescope that could detect changes in the strength of radio waves lasting a tiny fraction of a second.

The telescope recorded the twinkling as peaks and valleys that were traced out by a pen on rolls of special paper. The greatest number of scintillations occurred, as expected, during daylight hours when the telescope was pointed in the direction of the sun. But one day in August 1967, a pony-tailed graduate student from northern Ireland named Jocelyn Bell, who was responsible for monitoring the yards of tracings from the telescope, noticed something strange: the telescope had detected sharp, closely spaced peaks during nighttime observations. The alert young scientist suspected that the culprit was some local interference—perhaps the faulty ignition of a car. But the unusual pulses showed up night after night. No one at the observatory had seen anything like that before. For a while the signals vanished, but when they were detected again, the Cambridge team was able to make some astonishing measurements. These showed that the pulses occurred every 1.33731109 seconds. Whatever was causing the signals had an accuracy equaling that of some of the best clocks on earth.

Quickly eliminating the possibility of local interference as the source of the pulsations, the Cambridge astronomers determined that the waves had come from an area well beyond the limits of the solar system. Miss Bell was apparently the first to recognize this; for it was she who realized that the signals were of a sidereal nature—that is, they were coming from a source that rises and sets each day with the stars rather than the sun.

From the rapid rate at which the signals were being turned on and off, the Cambridge astronomers also realized that the source had to be quite small, perhaps no bigger than a planet like Mars. The first thought that crossed the minds of the scientists was that the signals might be messages from an extraterrestrial civilization. In fact, for a time, they only half jokingly called the signal source LGM1 (for Little Green Men). But as willing as most scientists are to acknowledge that our galaxy may be teeming with life—including advanced civilizations—the British radio astronomers soon dismissed this sensational possibility.

For one thing, LGM 1's estimated power output showed it was giving off as much energy as the sun. Even a civilization with more technological skills than ours would not squander energy at that rate, presumably. Furthermore, the signals were poorly chosen as message bearers; their frequency was so low they were nearly completely jammed by the radio noise of cosmic rays. And last, hard as the Cambridge astronomers looked, they could not find the slightest sign of any irregularity in the pulses; there was no indication that any messages had been imposed on the basic frequency. Reluctantly rejecting the designation LGM 1, the Cambridge team dubbed the pulsating signal source a pulsar, with the official name CP 1919 (for Cambridge pulsar and its sky position).

All through the investigations the British astronomers worked in an atmosphere of militarylike secrecy. Not even their colleagues at nearby Jodrell Bank were told of the discovery. Hewish and his associates were taking a calculated risk; if anyone else published any details about the strange signal source during their months of silence, the Cambridge team might lose the honor of discovering pulsars. But Hewish had a high-minded motive: he wanted to make sure that the signals were unmistakably a natural phenomenon, lest incomplete information give rise to wild rumors that an extraterrestrial civilization had been discovered.

By the time the Cambridge team announced its findings in a four-page article in the February 24, 1968, issue of the scientific journal *Nature,* there were no more doubts; the British radio astronomers had located three more pulsars. This made it even less probable that pulsars were of intelligent origin; for if one pulsar is a natural event, it is hardly likely that the others were being produced by intelligent beings.

Eliminating the possibility of intelligent origin of the signals, however, did not significantly lessen the puzzle facing scientists. They still did not know the nature of heavenly bodies that could flash on roughly once a second, give off a pulse of radio energy that lasted anywhere from a fiftieth to a twentieth of a second, and, for a brief moment, stand among the most powerful radio sources in the sky.

Planets could not be the cause because the signals would then have to have been created by intelligent creatures. Ordinary stars like the sun hardly seemed likely either. Nor could astronomers see how such variable stars as the Cepheids could produce such rapidly changing signals. Some scientists considered the possibility that the pulses might be coming from two stars in orbit around each other; as one star passed in front of its partner, momentarily blocking off some of its radiation, an observer on earth might pick up a brief change in signal strength. But no one could figure out how two stars could whirl around each other rapidly enough to produce pulses every second without ripping themselves apart.

Theorists eventually settled on two possibilities. One was a white dwarf. Under extreme conditions, they calculated, a white dwarf could spin as rapidly as once a second without destroying itself. But when radio astronomers at Green Bank, West Virginia, discovered a pulsar that was blinking on and off no fewer than 30 times a second, they had to abandon that theory. No white dwarf could rotate so rapidly. The newly discovered pulsar, which was found in the very heart of the Crab nebula, had to be something else. The only other possibility left was a neutron star.

The most powerful arguments in favor of that idea came from Thomas Gold of Cornell, who had been Hoyle's collaborator on the Steady State theory. An equally inventive theorist, Gold not only insisted that the Crab nebula pulsar was Fritz Zwicky's long-sought neutron star, but explained how such tiny bodies might give off periodic bursts of radiation.

According to Gold, charged particles were steadily leaking from one or more spots on the neutron star's surface. As they were thrown off into space by the star's rapid rotation, they were whipped to higher and higher speeds in great spiraling paths around the star by its whirling magnetic field. Finally approaching the velocity of light, the particles would give off synchrotron radiation; in effect, the star was acting like a giant particle accelerator.

To a distant observer on earth, the radiation would not come as a steady flow of energy. Since the particles whirl off from only one or perhaps two spots on the star, they form directional beams, like those from a lighthouse. It is only when one of those beams sweeps the earth as the star rotates that its radiation becomes detectable as pulses of radio noise.

Not all astronomers immediately accepted Gold's lighthouse model of pulsars; but it soon got strong support as a result of another discovery. Led by Cornell's Frank Drake, radio astronomers at Arecibo made extremely precise measurements of the Crab nebula pulsar and found it was slowing down 36.48 billionths of a second per day. Small as it was, the slowdown was readily explained by Gold's pulsar model and had indeed been predicted.

Gold pointed out that when the original star collapses, it quickly picks up rotational speed, like a spinning figure skater who pulls her arms in. But as the star throws off particles from its surface, it is also giving up energy. The loss makes itself apparent in a gradual loss of rotational speed. In fact, even though the slowdown is almost infinitesimally small in the case of the Crab nebula, physicists showed that it was just enough to account for all of the pulsar's radiation. On the other hand, if the neutron star were truly pulsating—swelling and contracting in size like a Cepheid variable—the pulses would occur increasingly rapidly as the star used up its energy. Besides, the neutron star theory of pulsars had predicted that pulsars might be found in the heart of supernovas. Since all known supernova remnants like the Crab would have to be relatively recent, in astronomical terms, they would contain young pulsars with very short pulse rate. All these conditions were seen in the Crab's pulsar.

Gold's pulsar model does not answer all questions about these strange blinking stars; but it seems to be the best and most widely accepted explanation. Moreover, as a result of Gold's work and that of other theorists, astronomers can describe a typical neutron star in fascinating detail.

The crust of the star is very solid, tougher than the strongest possible alloy. Furthermore, it is incredibly smooth; in contrast, a billiard ball as large as a neutron star would look as pockmarked as the moon. If any unevenness exists, the tiny "mountains" are no more than half an inch high. Because of the star's enormous gravitational pull, it would take more than the energy produced by a human in his entire lifetime to climb to the "mountain's" summit. Like the earth, the star is slightly wider at its equator because of its rapid rotation. But as the star slows down, this bulge flattens out and causes some cracking of the surface. In effect, there is a tiny starquake. The crustal movement may not amount to a shift of more than a ten-millionth of an inch, but because of the neutron star's great gravity, as much energy is released as if the surface of the earth crashed down 100 miles. During such fissuring, the star's spin rate rises briefly. As it happens, several temporary speedups in the Crab's pulsar have actually been observed; each lasted about 100 billionth of a second. Astronomers are reasonably certain that they were the result of starquakes.

Since the discovery of CP 1919 in 1967, radio astronomers have located more than 150 pulsars in the heavens. Significantly, all of them are slowing down. Besides radio waves, many of them also emit X rays, which can only be detected by rockets or satellites operating above the shielding atmosphere. In addition, the Crab nebula's powerful pulsar gives off high-energy gamma rays. In late 1974 University of Massachusetts radio astronomers reported an even stranger discovery: they picked up a set of double signals with the Arecibo dish that seemed to be two pulsars circling each other about once every eight hours. This celestial waltz, however, may not be unique. Many stars—perhaps a majority—are multiple stars: binaries, triplets or more complicated systems. Consequently, astronomers wonder why they have not found many more double pulsars. One possible explanation is that only a few pairs survive the powerful blast of a supernova, which may well blow away the small partner in the binary system.

Although pulsars are powerful radio beacons, only one pulsar has been positively identified with an optical telescope. This was verified with some ingenious photographic work by astronomers employing Lick Observatory's 120-inch mirror. On their camera they used a motion-picture-type shutter that rotated fast enough to catch the star between blinks. The technique produced a remarkable set of pictures that showed the star alternately switched on and off. The site of the flickering star was in the very center of the Crab nebula. A small, deep blue star, it had been pointed out as early as 1942 by Walter Baade and his colleague, Rudolph Minkowski, as the probable remnant of the great 1054 explosion that created the Crab nebula. Unaware that such stellar cadavers periodically dim out, however, astronomers had exposed all earlier photographs of the

Crab much too long to catch the star's brief bursts of light. Only when the alert Jocelyn Bell and her colleagues in Cambridge finally noticed a different kind of flickering from a different part of the sky could these extraordinary pulsing stars finally be detected.

12

LOOKING FOR
BLACK HOLES

In 1930 a talented young student from the University of Madras in India embarked by boat for England, where he hoped to continue his studies in physics at Cambridge University. To occupy himself during the long hours of a sea voyage nearly halfway around the world, Subrahmanyan Chandrasekhar did calculations on dying stars. Using Einstein's general relativity equations, he wanted to find out how far gravitational colcapse could continue—whether, for instance, it could crush a star into an even smaller and denser bundle than a white dwarf.

Chandrasekhar's calculations suggested that there could be further collapse, but in the paper that he later published on his shipboard work in *The Observatory Magazine* October 1934, he merely wrote that "one is left speculating on other possibilities" besides a white dwarf. The answer he had gotten was so wildly improbable he decided that no one in the scientific community would believe it if he made it public.

His fears proved to be well founded. Upon reading Chandrasekhar's paper, the British astronomer Arthur

Eddington pointed out that if a star kept contracting, its gravitational field would eventually become so powerful that not even light could escape from it. The star would become totally invisible. That idea had been suggested as far back as 1798, when Laplace said that a sufficiently dense body could not be seen because nothing could radiate from it. But more than a century later, Eddington considered such an outcome utterly unimaginable and, as a consequence, dismissed the young Chandrasekhar's reasoning as absurd.

Eddington's attitude was hardly untypical of his day. No one doubted that objects as compact as white dwarfs exist, because they had already been identified in the sky. But there was no direct evidence of smaller stars. The only hint that there might be denser objects came indirectly from observations of Zwicky and Baade showing that there were great stellar explosions in other galaxies (and presumably in our own too), although astronomers could merely speculate what such supernovas might leave behind.

Chandrasekhar's pioneering studies on stellar collapse were not totally ignored, however. In the next few years other scientists made further calculations. Interestingly, all of them were physicists who later went on to make key contributions to the development of the atomic and hydrogen bombs, which perhaps indicates that the study of something as remote as the awesome power of stars can help lead the way to terrifying practical results on earth. The distinguished roll call of scientists included Lev Landau, George Gamow, J. Robert Oppenheimer, and the Hungarian-born Edward Teller, who provided some of the key insights for the first American H-bomb.

Pondering the increasing strength of a collapsing star's gravity, they agreed that it could grow enormously powerful, even powerful enough to overcome the normal repulsive force between an atom's electrons and protons and form neutrons. But what would happen if the gravitational forces developed during collapse grew even larger? Would the tightly packed neutrons of a neutron star crush themselves into an even more bizarre form of matter? Tackling those questions, Oppenheimer, then a professor at the Berkeley campus of the University of California, and one of his students, Hartland Snyder, provided a stunning answer. They said that there was nothing in Einstein's equations that posed a barrier to further collapse. If the original mass of the star was great enough—say, three times that of the sun—the neutron star would be crushed.

During such a collapse, all the commonsense physical rules would be broken, producing what physicists call a singularity in space-time. As the star shrunk in size, its mass would become infinitely large, as would its gravitational force. Yet paradoxically, the star itself would occupy a spot in space so insignificant that it would be infinitely small. Inside the star, matter would lose its usual characteristics. Electrons and protons in the atoms would have ceased to exist, and would have been pounded together into neutrons. But as the star's density climbed further, finally exceeding 10 billion tons per cubic inch, the neutrons would be crushed into smaller fragments, and nothing could stop the collapse from continuing.

As the star's diameter became even smaller, time would slow down. Eventually even a fraction of a second would become an eternity. The idea of space would become meaningless. Light, of course, would not be able to escape this tightly packed gravitational world, nor would any other kind of electromagnetic radiation. To the relativity theorist, who sees gravity as a curving of space-time, the curvature would become so great that it would fold in upon itself, completely enveloping the star. It would become what the American physicist John A. Wheeler has called a "black hole" in space. Only the star's gravity, like the Cheshire cat's grin in *Alice's Adventures in Wonderland*, would be left behind to remind physicists of its former presence.

Anything near the black hole would feel its strong gravitational attraction. A spacecraft with powerful enough engines could perhaps approach quite close to a black hole, so long as it stayed outside its "absolute event horizon." This is the point of no return beyond which nothing can free itself from the black hole's grasp. It is sometimes also called the Schwarzchild radius after the German physicist Karl Schwarzschild, who first applied Einstein's general relativity equations to such singularities. For typical black holes the radius would be no more than 2 miles; note that the black hole itself has no boundaries in the usual sense.

If a beam of light passed close to the event horizon but did not cross it, it would go into orbit around the black hole. The region in which such a capture can occur is called the ergosphere (from the Greek *ergon,* meaning "work"). If nothing disturbs its path, the light can keep circling the collapsed star indefinitely.

Inside the black hole's event horizon, however, there is no chance of escape. If any object strays over it— whether a particle of light, an unlucky astronaut or spaceship, or even an entire planet—it will be completely swallowed up by the black hole. As the material tumbles downward, it will be simultaneously stretched and compressed; in short order, molecules and atoms will be ripped apart and even subnuclear particles will be destroyed beyond recognition. The entire process takes only a fraction of a second.

If a hapless spaceman tried to fight against this ultimate trip, he would only hasten his demise. For the harder he struggled the more energy he would expend; his mass, in turn, would become greater because mass and energy are equivalent, as would his gravitational field. As a result, his destruction would come all the quicker.

Such total devastation seems highly improbable. For it is one of the basic laws of physics that matter and/or energy can never be destroyed. Such laws apply to the observable universe. But the definition of a black hole as a singularity in space-time means that the conventional rules of physics and mathematics no longer have any meaning. It is a world completely beyond our experience. The material dropped into a black hole has entered another realm.

Because there are so many stars with masses significantly larger than the sun's, scientists suspect that there may be innumerable black holes in space. Some have even warned that in the future when spacecraft venture far beyond the solar system they will have to take into account the possibility that black holes may be unseen obstacles in their paths, like washed-out mountain roads that can quickly carry an unwary traveler to oblivion. In our galaxy alone, there could be millions of black holes. But if black holes give off no light or other radiation, how can they be detected?

If an observer got close enough to such a collapsing star, he might be able to see the star's light reddening as its waves stretched during their struggle to free themselves from the star's rising gravity before it blinks off completely. But even if he could watch the collapse from close up, it might all happen so quickly that he would see nothing more than a star suddenly disappearing from the sky.

Spotting the formation of a black hole from as far off as earth would be even more difficult—though scientists do not think such observations are entirely impossible. According to general relativity, the movement of any massive object through space, including a black hole, should be accompanied by a shower of gravitational energy, which Einstein said would come in the form of gravity waves or particles. Such waves would be the carriers of gravity, just as light waves are the carriers of electromagnetic energy.

For many years, a physicist at the University of Maryland, Joseph Weber, has been perfecting detectors, consisting of large aluminum cylinders, that are designed to respond to gravity's relatively weak radiation. In 1969, Weber announced that tiny movements he had picked up at the same instant in two widely separated cylinders were the result of the impact of gravity waves. Furthermore, he said, the waves seemed to be coming from the direction of the center of the galaxy. Packed with far more stars than the sun's sparsely populated stellar neighborhood, it could be the setting of many more star collapses, some of which could be giving off bursts of gravitational radiation.

Weber's work attracted worldwide attention, since it seemed to provide the first actual proof of Einstein's prediction about the existence of gravity waves half a century earlier. Other scientists, however, were unable to duplicate Weber's results when they set up gravity wave detectors of their own. The failure suggests that there may be something wrong with Weber's experiments—or those of his imitators. But it does not mean that Einstein was wrong and gravity waves do not exist or that black holes cannot produce them. Weber's difficulties only tend to confirm what physicists have long known: that gravity is the strongest of nature's basic forces at long range but still extremely hard to detect. Thus much more sensitive instruments may be needed to pick up gravity waves.

Astronomers, meanwhile, have suggested other methods of looking for black holes. One technique would involve examining multiple-star systems. In our galactic neighborhood astronomers have found hundreds of double and even triple stars, all of them bound together by mutual gravitational attraction. Such multiple-star systems can be detected even if only the largest star is visible in telescopes, because the unseen companion's gravity will affect the motion of the bigger star. To observers on earth, the visible star seems to be waltzing through space—tugged by a partner whose presence is felt but not seen. From these erratic movements, astronomers can determine the mass of the unseen companion. If the mass is at least three times that of the sun, they can reasonably conclude that the unseen companion may be a black hole.

They would still not be certain and would need other evidence to confirm their suspicions. But can there be other clues when the black hole is invisible? In 1967 two Russian astrophysicists, Yakov Zel'dovich and I. D. Novikov, pointed out that the black hole's powerful gravity would not only tug on its partner, but pull it into an egg shape and draw off large quantities of the visible star's gases. Spiraling toward the black hole, the particles in these gases would collide and compress together—so violently, in fact, that they would eventually heat up to temperatures of 100 million degrees K. The heat would be so great that it would produce a flood of high-energy X rays and gamma rays. To an observer on earth, the rays would seem to come in bursts. As the black hole passed behind the visible star while orbiting it, the rays would be briefly blocked off, as in an ordinary eclipse.

Neither X rays nor gamma rays from space can be observed on earth because the earth's atmosphere acts as a shield against such radiation, which must be detected from a platform high above the earth. The first serious efforts to measure such radiation from space began in 1949, when Herbert Friedman of the Naval Research Laboratory in Washington began sending up captured German V-2 rockets from World War II equipped with X-ray detectors. In these experiments, he found that the sun is a powerful X-ray emitter, especially during the fiery eruption of solar flares. Later, scientists noticed that the entire sky teems with X rays even when the sun's surface is relatively quiet. Something other than the sun has to be producing the X rays.

Trying ot track down the mysterious source of these emissions, scientists launched more rockets equipped with better detectors that were able to locate the direction from which the X rays were coming. Some seemed to be originating in the center of the galaxy; others from the constellation Scorpius. Hence the source became known as Scorpius X-1 (indicating that it was the first X-ray source to be discovered in that constellation). Another powerful X-ray source, Taurus X-1, was found in the Crab nebula. Eventually so many sources were found that they encouraged the birth of a new form of stargazing called X-ray astronomy. For serious studies in X-ray astronomy, rockets were inadequate. They could provide only a fleeting glimpse of the X-ray source, lasting no longer than a few minutes. For extended viewing X-ray astronomers needed satellites that remained in orbit for long periods.

The first such satellite was launched by the National Space and Aeronautics Administration (NASA) in 1970 from a platform off the coast of Kenya on the seventh anniversary of the East African nation's independence. In honor of that occasion the satellite was dubbed *Uhuru,* the word for "freedom" in Swahili. *Uhuru* was a remarkably successful instrument. Slowly rotating once every 12 minutes high above the earth, the satellite regularly swept the sky with its X-ray telescope and radioed its findings to a control center on the ground, directed by Riccardo Giacconi and his fellow X-ray astronomers in Cambridge, Massachusetts. In a year and a half of operation *Uhuru* pinpointed no fewer than 161 X-ray sources in the sky.

Of these, at least two appeared to be part of binary star systems, Centaurus X-3 and Hercules X-1, in which one of the partners seemed to be a neutron star. The X rays arrived precisely every 4.84239 seconds from Centaurus X-1 and every 1.23782 seconds from Hercules X-1. Like black holes, the neutron stars were presumed to be pulling gases from their larger companions because of the great gravity of these tiny bodies. But there the similarity with black holes ended. The gases were funneled down the lines of magnetic force surrounding the neutron star; black holes, on the other hand, do not have magnetic fields around them since by definition all electromagnetic energy remains trapped inside of them. As the gases approached the neutron star, they would also be heated up to temperatures high enough to create X rays, but because of the magnetic field they would be sharply focused into a beam rather than being dispersed in all directions. As the beam swept the sky during the neutron star's lighthouselike rotation the emerging X rays would periodically cross the path of the earth and register in *Uhuru*'s instruments. Lacking a magnetic field, black holes could not produce X rays in quite this way. In addition, pulses coming from black holes could not be as short as those from Centaurus X-1 or Hercules X-1, since it seems inconceivable that a black hole could sweep around its companion in only a few seconds.

Even though Centaurus X-1 and Hercules X-1 did not seem to be black holes, the new catalogue of X-ray sources included another highly suspicious emitter, Cygnus X-1. After *Uhuru* had roughly pinpointed the source in the constellation Cygnus, radio astronomers aimed their telescopes at the area and got a better fix from its radio emissions. Finally, optical astronomers turned their instruments at the region and found a huge star, a "class 3 supergiant giant," designated HDE 226868, which was equal to at least twenty solar masses. It was moving erratically through space, apparently tugged by an unseen companion. From these movements, astronomers calculated that the supergiant, which was some 8000 light years away, had a partner of three solar masses or more. That size was large enough to fall within the mass limits of a black hole.

More evidence came in 1973 from another X-ray satellite named *Copernicus* (in honor of the 500th anniversary of the Polish scientist's birth). Equipped with more precise detectors, *Copernicus* determined that the X rays from Cygnus X-1 were sharply decreasing every 5.6 days. According to the spectral studies of the optical astronomers, the interval precisely matched the time it takes the supergiant's unseen companion to make one swing around its larger partner.

For astronomers everywhere the picture suddenly became clear. Every 5.6 days the black hole apparently passed behind the supergiant, which briefly cut off the flow of X rays—thereby accounting for the periodic fluctuations in X-ray strength picked up by *Copernicus*. While the case was far from proved, the observations added up to the best evidence yet for the existence of a black hole.

Since then, Giacconi's team, which is now part of the Harvard-Smithsonian Center for Astrophysics, has identified a second possible black hole in another X-ray source, Circinus X, in the southern hemisphere's skies. At Circinus X's apparent location, Australian optical astronomers have found a dim red star that may be experiencing the tug of an unseen companion's large gravity. Another black-hole candidate is Cygnus X-3, whose periodic X-ray emissions suddenly fl   at least 200 times in strength in September 1972. Some astronomers think that the dramatic increase may have been the result of a supernova.

In recent years theorists have suggested that black holes may also come in even tinier packages as a result of a process other than the collapse of a dying star. According to the British astrophysicist Stephen Hawking, these mini black holes would be no bigger than a virus but would carry as much mass as an asteroid. They would have been formed at the very start of the universe during the Big Bang. As Hawking sees it, the great explosion could have created pockets of high compression where material would have been sufficiently squeezed to create tiny black holes, some of which may still be drifting through space. Taking up Hawking's idea, some scientists have pointed out that the mysterious fireball that leveled a large area in the Tunguska region of Siberia in 1908 may have been such a mini black hole, although the conventional explanation for the disaster has been a hit by a stray comet or meteorite. Other scientists have even proposed that mini black holes, if they exist, might be "captured" and towed to the earth's vicinity. If an orbital power plant was erected around such a black hole, its virtually limitless energy could perhaps be tapped and beamed to earth.

Most scientists do not take such proposals very seriously. In fact, many of them are not absolutely convinced that black holes exist. They point out, for instance, that there may be other explanations for the burst-like behavior of the X rays from Cygnus X-1 and similar sources. Giacconi himself concedes: "It would be difficult to prove the existence of this new class of objects with only one example." But as many astronomers point out, if the observations are not the result of black holes, there must be something at least as strange out there.

13

THE FATE
OF THE UNIVERSE

The Big Bang theory says that the universe was born some 10 to 20 billion years ago in the explosion of a densely packed, extremely hot ball of primordial matter. As the gases flew off in all directions from the site of the great blast, some gas began to cool and contract into galaxies and stars. But even as cooling was taking place, the galaxies continued their outward flight away from each other. Numerous signs in the sky confirm such a scenario, ranging from the red shifts of distant galaxies to the more recent detection of faint microwave radiation that may be the faint glow left over from the cataclysmic explosion.

But for reasons that seem as much philosophical as theoretical, many astronomers cannot believe that the expansion that is now being observed will continue forever. They contend that the outward flight of the galaxies will gradually slow down, halt, and reverse itself, like a ball that descends after being tossed into the air. When that reversal occurs, all the parts of the universe—galaxies, stars, and planets, and even interstellar dust—will come crashing together again.

In 1960, after studying the rate at which the galaxies were flying apart—a rate he determined from their red shifts—Palomar astronomer Allan Sandage gave a timetable for the life of the universe. According to his tentative estimates, the entire process from Big Bang to reversal of the outward flight of the galaxies to ultimate collapse would take 80 billion years. Sandage's figure certainly did not present an immediate threat, since we are no more than a fourth of the way through the universe's predicted lifetime; but it did pose a challenge to astronomers.

If the universe's expansion is really slowing down significantly, what is causing that slowdown? The answer obviously is gravity, the glue that binds the universe together. Yet, hard as astronomers have looked, they have not found nearly enough mass to provide the needed gravitational braking force for the slowdown. In fact, based on Newton's well-known law that the gravity exerted by any body is proportional to its mass, there should be about ten times as much mass in the universe as astronomers seem able to find in their telescopes.

Perhaps the most vivid example of the missing mass problem is connected with observations of galactic clusters. Although the universe is filled with millions upon millions of galaxies, they are not distributed at random but in groupings called clusters. The Milky Way, as has been pointed out, is a member of such a cluster. Within the clusters, individual galaxies move at great speeds with respect to each other, apart from the general expansion of the universe. These movements, in fact, are so rapid that the clusters should long ago have broken apart. They are clearly bound together by gravity, yet the mass observed in these clusters is only about 10 percent of that required to keep them intact.

Some scientists have suggested that the missing mass is hidden in the great clouds of matter between the stars or even in the giant halos that seem to surround galaxies. The most intriguing possibility is that the mass may really be missing—inside black holes. Although hidden from sight, the mass would make itself felt through its gravitational influence.

Such solutions to the case of the missing mass, however, are not accepted by every scientist. Pondering the ultimate fate of the universe, the nonbelievers have come to a different conclusion. Not only do they doubt that enough mass is packed away in black holes or anywhere else to provide the braking force; they cite other negative evidence that touches on the nature of the Big Bang. That evidence is the unexpectedly large amounts of deuterium recently found in space by satellites and radio telescopes. As noted, deuterium is an isotope of hydrogen that has, in addition to its single proton, a neutron in its nucleus. Scientists had assumed that deuterium is forged in the thermonuclear fires of stars, the source of most atoms. But such large quantities of deuterium have been uncovered lately that it could not have been formed in the stars. Instead, the source probably was the Big Bang. Yet, curiously, if the great explosion was as powerful as most theorists say, it should have fused most of the deuterium into heavier nuclei of helium. From this evidence, Caltech's James E. Gunn and other astronomers have come to a startling conclusion: they say that not only was the Big Bang's fireball smaller and less powerful than has been thought, but the universe is less dense than earlier estimates by "closed" universe theorists suggest. Such theorists are persuaded that there is enough available mass to reverse the expansion, and predict that the universe will literally close in on itself.

In his arguments against a closed universe, Gunn found an unexpected ally in Sandage. In 1974, after long observations of distant galaxies with a colleague, the Swiss-born astronomer Gustav Tammann, Sandage announced a new figure for the Hubble constant, which in turn meant a revised age for the universe, about 16 billion years. Even more interesting, Sandage disclosed that he did not find the slowdown in the universe's expansion that had been suggested by his earlier work.

To understand how Sandage came to his conclusion, it must be remembered that the telescope can be considered as a time machine. In looking at distant galaxies with the 200-inch Palomar mirror, he was also looking far back into time. A galaxy that is 3 billion light-years away is also at least 3 billion years old, since the light we are now seeing began its journey toward us that long ago. Similarly, the velocity of the galaxy deduced from its red shift is actually its speed at an earlier age of the universe, closer to the time of the Big Bang. In that earlier period of the universe, the galaxy's speed should have been greater than that of closer—or younger—galaxies. Thus, by comparing the speeds of nearby galaxies with those of more distant galaxies, Sandage could calculate the extent of any slowdown in the universe's expansion.

The results were startling. At odds with his earlier measurements that indicated the universe would come to an end some 80 billion years after the Big Bang, the new observations suggested that the expansion would go on forever, and that the universe was "open."

Sandage himself accepted the evidence with considerable reluctance. "This expansion is such a strange conclusion," he commented in an interview in *Time*, "one's first assumption is that it cannot really be true, and yet it is the premier fact." Gunn also found it difficult, and even contradictory, to envision a universe of finite parts expanding eternally into an infinite volume. "Imagine," he said, "even though the density of its mass is small, the total amount of mass is infinite because space is infinitely big."

Needless to say, these findings caused considerable debate. Closed universe theorists point out that the observational data are at best imprecise, and can be interpreted in other ways. They also seem to defy the intuitive feeling that the universe somehow must have limits. Thus, in spite of the difficulties of a closed universe theory, many scientists are persuaded that the expansion will eventually end.

That would not only bring all the parts of the universe flying together again, but, in the opinion of some imaginative theorists, would also cause other fantastic events to happen. As the galaxies moved closer, the direction of time would be reversed, like a film played backward in a motion-picture projector. Instead of giving off light, the stars would absorb it. Eventually they would break down completely, their elements distintegrating into the hydrogen gas out of which they were originally made. To the outside observer (if one could exist), life processes would also reverse. People would get younger rather than older, and wind up in the womb rather than in the grave. As the galaxies approached each other, the sky would be ablaze with light (although not from individual stars), and life would end. Finally, all the components of the universe would vaporize each other, and all that would be left of the galaxies, stars, and planets would be a hot, dense fireball.

Some astronomers say that the universe will then begin anew, exploding in another Big Bang. As the material from the explosion flows outward, galaxies and stars will form again and even life will reemerge. But eventually the expansion will halt and another collapse will occur, bringing about a new universe. Such a cycle of expansion, contraction, and expansion is called an oscillating universe. It too envisions no beginning or end, although the universe never becomes infinite in size.

Other scientists, like John Wheeler, believe that the entire universe will collapse into a black hole. But even that collapse may not be as final as it seems. We have assumed so far that black holes are perfectly spherical and at rest. But experience tells astronomers that neither stars nor galaxies are perfect spheres, nor are they motionless. When such objects contract, their lumps and other distortions tend to become more exaggerated. As a result, the object might not be totally crushed into oblivion; not all sides would be completely sealed off. If the collapse took an uneven course, theorists say that the black hole would change its position relative to the universe; it might even become a tunnel—or wormhole, as theorists call it—to some different point in space and time. Strange as it seems, it might become a passageway to another universe.

The idea is not dismissed by theorists. Wheeler, for one, thinks that our universe may only be one of an infinity of universes in a strange realm that he calls "superspace." Almost as much a poetical notion as a mathematical one, superspace does not have the traditional four dimensions—the three dimensions of ordinary space, plus time; it has an infinite number of dimensions. Unlike our universe, superspace has no beginning and no end. In this eternal world our universe of galaxies and stars is only a speck, a point in space and time. Wheeler himself compares superspace to a huge arena with many stages. The drama of our universe—its birth, expansion, and death—is played on one of these stages, yet the stage provides only a setting. Elsewhere in the arena of superspace, the drama of other universes may be unfolding on other stages.

If black holes are tunnels to other points in time and space, some scientists have suggested that in the future they could perhaps be used to conquer the enormous distances of space. Such speculations sound like the "space warps" imagined by science fiction writers, but the idea that different parts of our universe or even other universes may be connected by a network of wormholes has been considered by serious scientists. Some have even suggested that such tunnels may be at the root of the mystery of quasars, which seem to be giving off energy at rates totally out of proportion to their size. In the view of these scientists, the brilliantly glowing quasars may be the exit ports for stars and even galaxies that have collapsed in other universes and are emerging in our own. Such exit ports are called white holes.

Considerable skepticism exists among physicists

about such theories, as it also does about the existence of black holes. For instance, the doubters point out, so much material may be blown off during a supernova or any other cataclysmic collapse that not enough mass is left to form a black hole. But if there are no black holes, this would present equally serious problems. Certainly Einstein's gravity equations would have to be scrapped or drastically revised. As physicists like to joke: either there are holes in the sky, or there are holes in the general theory of relativity.

Wheeler does not think there are holes in relativity. Envisioning the formation of a black hole as only a preview of the universe's own collapse, he argues that our world will be so thoroughly compressed that it will be squeezed, in Wheeler's phrase, through a knothole in space and emerge as something entirely different. In this new universe, fundamental quantities like the size and shape of nuclear particles—the basic building blocks of matter—will be unrecognizable, as will be such physical constants as the speed of light or the acceleration of gravity. Like clouds formed after a violent storm, the reborn universe will take on an entirely new configuration. But, says Wheeler, even this new world will not be permanent. It is also destined to collapse in time and to be reborn in a different form, and so the universes will come and go in a march toward infinity.

That at least is the grand vision of John Wheeler and his colleagues. Almost mystical in conception, these ideas show how close science and religion have become. Both are trying to unravel basic mysteries. How did the universe begin? How will it end? Is there any existence beyond the end? The questions themselves may never be answered with certainty, but even in asking them, man is likely to learn more about himself, his world, and his destiny. That alone makes them highly worthwhile.

GLOSSARY

Absolute event horizon. The theoretical boundary of a black hole past which nothing can escape.

Absolute magnitude. The actual brightness of a star when viewed from a distance arbitrarily set at 32.6 light-years.

Absolute zero. The temperature ($-460°$ Fahrenheit or $-273°$ centigrade) that represents the total absence of heat.

Accelerator. A form of atom smasher in which atomic particles are accelerated to extremely high velocities before they hit their target atoms.

Antimatter. Matter that appears identical to ordinary matter except that its basic characteristics are reversed. For example, the electron has a negative charge; its antimatter counterpart, the positron, has a positive charge.

Apparent magnitude. The brightness of a star as it appears on earth.

Asteroid. One of the thousands of chunks of matter circling the sun chiefly between the orbits of Mars and Jupiter.

Astrology. A pseudoscience that holds to the ancient view that the planets and stars directly influence our daily lives.

Astronomy. The study of heavenly bodies by observation and theory.

Astrophysics. A branch of astronomy that is concerned with the physical processes at work in the universe, especially in the interiors of stars.

Atom. The smallest unit of an element such as hydrogen or carbon.

Big Bang. The cataclysmic explosion that many astronomers believe marked the birth of the universe.

Binary star. One of a pair of stars circling a common center of gravity.

Black hole. A massive star that has collapsed so completely after running out of nuclear fuel that its enormous gravity allows nothing to escape—not even light; hence it is invisible.

Closed universe. The view that the current expansion of the universe will eventually stop and reverse itself.

Comets. Small chunks of matter—probably consisting of icy debris—that travel through the solar system in highly elongated orbits and develop bright tails when they approach the sun.

Constellation. A group of stars that, in the eyes of the ancients, formed recognizable images.

Cosmic rays. Energetic particles consisting mostly of protons.

Cosmology. The study of the origin and development of the universe.

Doppler effect. The apparent change in the wavelength or frequency of light or sound resulting from the motion of its source toward or away from an observer. See *Red shift.*

Electromagnetic radiation. Any radiation produced by changing electric or magnetic fields—for example, visible light.

Exobiology. The study of extraterrestrial life.

Extraterrestrial. Beyond the earth.

Fission. The splitting of the atomic nucleus; the process at work in nuclear reactors or atomic bombs.

Fusion. The combination of atomic nuclei to form heavier nuclei; the process that powers stars and the hydrogen bomb.

Galaxy. A huge island of stars in space bound together by their gravitational attraction.

Gamma rays. Electromagnetic radiation of the shortest wavelength.

Gravity. The basic force exerted by all matter.

Gravity (or gravitational) waves. The carrier of gravitational energy through space.

Hertzsprung-Russell diagram. A method of plotting the absolute magnitude of stars against their temperature or spectral type.

Hubble constant. The number that describes the relationship between the velocities of receding galaxies and their distance; the figure can be used to calculate the time elapsed since the Big Bang.

Infrared radiation. Light that has a wavelength slightly longer than visible red light.

Isotope. One of the various forms of an element. Isotopes of the same element have the same number of protons in their nuclei but a different number of neutrons.

Light-year. The distance that light, traveling at a speed of about 186,000 miles per second, traverses in a year: roughly 6 trillion miles.

Local group. The cluster of twenty or so nearby (astronomically speaking) galaxies, of which the Milky Way is a member.

Magnitude. The brightness of a star, galaxy, or other heavenly body.

Main sequence. The wide band across the Hertzsprung-Russell diagram on which most ordinary stars are found during most of their lives.

Meteoroid. A small chunk of matter moving through space; when such a bit of debris appears in the earth's atmosphere, it is called a meteor ("shooting star"). If it survives its flaming plunge through the earth's atmosphere it becomes a meteorite.

Milky Way. The name given by the ancients to the band of starlight that circles the sky; now used by astronomers as the name of our galaxy. Shaped like a disk, the galaxy appears as a band across the heavens because of the solar system's position in its outer fringes.

Molecule. Two or more atoms linked by chemical bonds.

Nebula. Any blurred or diffuse light source in the sky. Although the term was once applied to objects inside and outside the Milky Way, it is now commonly restricted to gaseous dusty clouds inside the Milky Way—for example, the Crab nebula and the Orion nebula.

Neutron. Elementary particle that is one of the building blocks of the atom's nucleus. Neutrons are electrically neutral.

Neutron star. An extremely small but massive collapsed star composed entirely of neutrons.

Nova. A star that suddenly increases in brightness by a factor of 100 or more.

Open universe. The view of some cosmologists that the universe is destined to expand eternally.

Orbit. The path of a body as it travels through space under the influence of the gravity of another body.

Planet. From the Greek word for "wanderer." Now applied to any large cold body in orbit around a central star.

Plasma. A hot, electrically charged gas. Often called the fourth state of matter along with solids, liquids, and ordinary uncharged gases.

Proton. Along with the neutron, one of the two primary elementary particles that form the nucleus of the atom. It has a positive electric charge.

Pulsar. A small, rapidly fluctuating source of radio waves that astronomers believe has a neutron star at its center.

Quasar. An apparently starlike (or quasi-stellar) object that may be extremely distant and brighter than whole galaxies of stars.

Radioactivity. The breakdown of certain atoms into lighter atoms accompanied by the release of particles and energy.

Radio astronomy. The branch of astronomy that deals with the study of radio sources, which can be planets, stars, galaxies, or quasars.

Red giant. A huge expanded star (like Betelgeuse in the constellation Orion) that has a diameter many times that of the sun.

Red shift. A shift in the wavelength of light toward the red end of the spectrum. When observed in galaxies, it is usually seen as a sign that the galaxy is speeding away from us.

Solar wind. The steady stream of charged particles coming from the sun.

Spectrum. The separation of light into its component wavelengths.

Star. Now means any self-luminous body fired by thermonuclear reactions.

Steady State. A theory of the universe that holds it has no beginning or end; that matter is continuously created throughout it; and that the universe's properties do not change over time or distance.

Sunspot. A darker, relatively cool patch on the sun's surface.

Supernova. A stellar explosion so violent that the star may shine as brightly as its entire galaxy.

Thermonuclear energy. The energy produced by fusion reactions in a star or H-bomb.

Ultraviolet radiation. Light that has a wavelength slightly shorter than visible violet light.

Universe. All of space, matter, energy, and time.

White dwarf. A small, earth-sized collapsed star; believed to be what will finally become of the sun.

White hole. The reverse of a black hole; instead of trapping energy and matter, it spills it out.

X rays. A form of radiation that lies between the ultraviolet and gamma ray wavelengths.

SELECTED BIBLIOGRAPHY

BOOKS

Bergmann, Peter G. *The Riddle of Gravitation*. New York: Charles Scribner's Sons, 1968. Lucid explanation of general relativity for the layman with a minimum of mathematical training.

Brandt, John C., and Maran, Stephen P. *New Horizons in Astronomy*. San Francisco: W. H. Freeman and Co., 1972. A well-written basic astronomy text for nonscience majors that incorporates many of astronomy's new ideas.

Calder, Nigel. *Violent Universe*. New York: Viking Press, 1969. Richly illustrated, lively account of the author's tour of leading observatories.

Dickson, F. P. *The Bowl of Night*. Cambridge, Mass.: M.I.T. Press, 1968. An introduction to modern cosmology for nonscience college students.

Goldsmith, Donald, and Levy, Donald. *From the Black Hole to the Infinite Universe*. San Francisco: Holden-Day, 1974. A clever basic college physics text that mixes science fact with chapter introductions that are science fiction.

149

Hoyle, Fred. *Nicolaus Copernicus*. New York: Harper & Row, 1973. The noted British scientist's clear elucidation of Copernicus's theory on the occasion of the 500th anniversary of his birth.

Jastrow, Robert. *Red Giants and White Dwarfs*. (Rev. ed.) New York: Harper & Row, 1969. Highly readable account of the origin of the sun and its planets as well as the emergence of life on one of them.

John, Laurie (ed.). *Cosmology Now*. London: British Broadcasting Corporation, 1973. Based on radio talks by some of today's leading astronomers and cosmologists. Roger Penrose's chapter on black holes (p. 103) is especially notable.

Kaufmann, William J., III. *Relativity and Cosmology*. New York: Harper & Row, 1973. A concise explanation of some of the new problems in astronomy.

Lovell, Bernard. *Out of the Zenith*. New York: Harper & Row, 1973. Somewhat technical account of contemporary radio astronomy by the scientist who led the construction of Britain's big Jodrell Bank dish.

Munitz, Milton K. (ed.). *Theories of the Universe*. New York: Free Press, 1957. Intriguing selections on man's views of the universe from the ancient Babylonians to contemporary cosmologist Fred Hoyle.

Pfeiffer, John. *The Changing Universe*. New York: Random House, 1956. Recapitulation of radio astronomy's beginnings, including good biographical details on pioneers Karl Jansky and Grote Reber.

Saslow, William C., and Jacobs, Kenneth C. (eds.). *The Emerging Universe*. Charlottesville: University Press of Virginia, 1972. Lectures by leading astronomers on such contemporary topics as pulsars, Big Bang cosmology, and chemistry between the stars. Technical in parts.

Sciama, D. W. *Modern Cosmology*. London: Cambridge University Press, 1971. Discussion of such topics as stars, galaxies, radio galaxies, and quasars by a leading theorist. Clear but occasionally technical.

Scientific American. *The Universe*. New York: Simon and Schuster, 1956. Readings from the noted magazine on the origins, shape, and structural details of the universe by such distinguished scientists as Walter Baade, George Gamow, and Martin Ryle.

Shklovskii, I. S., and Sagan, Carl. *Intelligent Life in the Universe*. New York: Dell Publishing Co., 1966. An unusual collaboration by a Soviet and an American astronomer that not only speculates on extraterrestrial life but provides a readable account of contemporary astronomy.

Taylor, John G. *Black Holes: The End of the Universe?* New York: Random House, 1973. Lively, controversial speculations about the ultimate collapse.

Verschuur, Gerrit L. *The Invisible Universe*. New York: Springer-Verlag, 1974. An introduction to radio astronomy for laymen.

Whitney, Charles A. *The Discovery of Our Galaxy*. New York: Alfred A. Knopf, 1971. Highly readable retelling of how our picture of the Milky Way emerged. Includes good account of the work of Edwin P. Hubble.

ARTICLES

Asimov, Isaac. "Gravitation Unlimited." *International Wildlife,* Nov.-Dec. 1974, pp. 33–37. Explanation of black holes in the inimitable Asimov style.

Drake, Frank D. "The Astounding Pulsars." *Science Year,* 1970, pp. 37–51. Nontechnical account of the discovery of pulsars by a well-known radio astronomer.

Logan, Jonothan L. "Gravitational Waves: A Progress Report." *Physics Today,* March 1973, pp. 44–52. Somewhat technical discussion of attempts to detect gravitational radiation.

Maran, Stephen P. "The Crab Nebula Mystery." *Smithsonian*, June 1970, pp. 51–57. Popular account of how the Crab was identified as a pulsar.

Morrison, Philip. "Resolving the Mystery of the Quasars?" *Physics Today*, March 1973, pp. 23–29. The eminent physicist's ideas about quasars.

Ostriker, Jeremiah P. "The Nature of Pulsars." *Scientific American*, Jan. 1971, pp. 48–60. A more scientific account of the discovery and identification of pulsars.

Penrose, Roger. "Black Holes." *Scientific American*, May 1972, pp. 38–46. Good lay introduction to the theory of black holes.

Ruffini, Remo, and Wheeler, John A. "Introducing the Black Hole." *Physics Today*, Jan. 1971, pp. 30–41. Perhaps difficult, but worth the extra effort for the serious reader.

Scientific American. Issue on the Solar System, Sept. 1975. Articles by Carl Sagan and others on the new knowledge about the sun and the objects in orbit around it.

Sullivan, Walter. "A Hole in the Sky." *New York Times Magazine*, July 14, 1974, pp. 11–35. A nontechnical account of the speculations about black holes.

Thorne, Kip S. "The Search for Black Holes." *Scientific American*, Dec. 1974, pp. 32–43. Techniques for finding black holes.

Wheeler, John A. "Beyond the Black Hole." *Science Year*, 1975, pp. 76–89. The noted physicist's futuristic tale of an encounter with a black hole.

ILLUSTRATION CREDITS

INDEX